Strategic Cost
Transformation

Strategic Cost Transformation

Using Business Domain Management to Improve Cost Data, Analysis, and Management

Reginald Tomas Lee

BEP BUSINESS EXPERT PRESS

Strategic Cost Transformation: Using Business Domain Management to Improve Cost Data, Analysis, and Management

First published in 2019 by
Business Expert Press, LLC
222 East 46th Street, New York, NY 10017
www.businessexpertpress.com

ISBN-13: 978-1-63157-879-3 (paperback)
ISBN-13: 978-1-63157-880-9 (e-book)

Business Expert Press Managerial Accounting Collection

Collection ISSN: 2152-7113 (print)
Collection ISSN: 2152-7121 (electronic)

Cover and interior design by Exeter Premedia Services Private Ltd., Chennai, India

First edition: 2019

10 9 8 7 6 5 4 3 2 1

Printed in the United States of America.

To Marc (my brother)

Abstract

Whether considered a goal or an objective, one thing is for certain; to survive and thrive, companies need to make money. To be effective at making money, employees need tools, models, and insights that lead to decisions that enable improved cash generation. We typically look to and rely on accounting information as a basis for these analyses and the resulting decisions.

In my last book, *Lies, Damned Lies, and Cost Accounting*, I argued cost accounting is ill-equipped to provide cash information about a company. It wasn't a knock on cost accounting. Instead, it pointed out we are asking cost accounting to do something and provide information it wasn't designed for.

Upon reading *Lies*, many asked, "If cost accounting isn't what we should use for cash information, what *should* we use?" Enter Business Domain Management, or BDM. BDM is an organizational and financial framework that breaks companies into two business domains, the Operations and Cash or OC Domain and the Accounting Domain. The OC Domain is where business and cash transactions occur; where work happens, and money is spent and received. It is in the OC Domain where we make decisions that affect the rate cash enters and leaves the company, and it is here where we know if we have made money or not, before we've calculated a single cost. The Accounting Domain is where we account for what happened in the OC Domain. This is where we traditionally looked for cash data.

The BDM framework provides a powerful model for understanding operational and financial performance in its entirety, and it far exceeds anything accounting can provide on its own. Strategic Cost Transformation takes you on a journey from focusing on accounting information to having a corporate-wide model that creates alignment between areas in companies where there is usually misalignment—operations, cash, and accounting.

Keywords

BCR; business cash requirements; capacity management; cash; cost reduction; costs; efficiency; effectivity; input capacity; isocash curve; metrics; optimization; output capacity; product profitability; productivity; profit

Contents

Testimonials

As a CPA with over 30 years of accounting experience, I certainly had to swallow my pride as I read this book. Dr. Lee provides compelling evidence that you cannot rely on accounting information alone to make cash decisions.

—Michael Hales
Chief Financial Officer
Northern Kentucky University

Epictetus, a Greek Stoic philosopher, is reported to have said that many things in this world are not and yet appear to be. Such is the case with many of our traditional definitions and descriptions of "cost savings" as described in so many accounting texts. Dr. Lee has taken a page from Epictetus in pointing out that we need a new paradigm of defining a "cost saving" if we are going to really provide the necessary information needed to manage a business or use accounting information to make more informed business decisions. This book is clearly a game changer in that regard.

—Dr. Joseph F. Castellano
Professor Emeritus, University of Dayton

Dr. Lee has committed to educating business executives in a way that drives real, generational change. Strategic Cost Transformation is written to accomplish just that. We all want to get to the future ahead of our competitors and to be the early adaptors of the next wave of change, and this highly effective roadmap moves us immediately from idea to reality in a surprisingly doable way. When I first saw Reginald present his ideas, I immediately knew there was something necessary and urgent to his ideas that my company needed to implement. Strategic Cost Transformation is outstanding and does not disappoint. As a lifelong accountant and businessman it energizes me to bring my team's talents and experiences to become more deeply involved with operating processes and cash flows, thereby creating exceptional profitability and competitive advantage.

—Steve Zofkie
Chief Financial Officer, Applied Mechanical Systems, Inc.

Technology has fundamentally changed our role with clients, the way we show up to execute that role, and also our responsibility to create, capture, and communicate value.

In this new world, the training, mindset, skills, approaches, and experience that got us to where we are now are not going to get us to where we need to be. Cost accounting might make sense in a 2D transactional world where we are focused purely on metrics and understanding what has transpired in the past. In that realm, we got some comfort from tracking time (efficiency) and creating subjective mathematical relationships that only matter to us, not our clients.

Cost accounting has become a kind of anesthesia for not having the impact and results that we must have in order to remain relevant to our clients. We now find ourselves in the business of relationships and this requires us to find new measurements and drivers that are meaningful and create real impact and value in the eyes of our clients. Many authors have posited that cost accounting is not relevant but Dr. Lee is the first to prove it mathematically and offer the replacement, which is cash flow management based on objective data from the operational realm. If you are an accountant or studying to become one, I recommend this book to you highly.

—Rhondalynn Korolak
Lawyer, accountant, best-selling author, advisory expert and Managing
Director of businest® and Make the SHIFT™

Traditional cost accounting didn't hold much allure for me and still doesn't. After my introduction to activity-based costing and the theory of constraints almost 30 years ago, I thought the path was clear to begin adding true value to the enterprise using these disciplines as an AND rather than an OR for better systems thinking, better internal decision making and to make money. I successfully focused primarily on enterprise-wide process cost measurements for the next 30 years in the service industry, building ever more strategic, financial and operational deliverables. However, my Quixotic adventures to leverage ABC methodologies into cash and capacity analysis were particularly challenging and victories came at great costs. I needed a better solution. This book provides that solution—lighting the way through an important new discipline and understanding focused on separating cash and capacity to operations analyses from those that focus on cost accounting measurements. Dr. Lee's book is recommended reading for every FP&A department with a mission of aligning its resources to the enterprise's corporate goals and objectives.

—Jeff Enyart

Former Second Vice President, Finance & FP&A

Ohio National Financial Services

I've been an Operations Controller for the past 15 years and actively involved in manufacturing for the past 25 year. After reading Dr. Lee's book the word anticipation comes to my mind. Finance must understand where the operations will end up after strategy and operational performance, execution. As a result we need to anticipate where, what, and when our companies will meet their targets, and most importantly, if those decisions will lead us to a favorable cash position. As well the book provides a comprehensive approach on how to dissect accounting and operational performance measures, measures that accounting will not support for the new CFO's role we are living.

—Luis Manuel Hernández

CEO, KMCM Consulting Services, Inc.

Secretary and Member of the Board of México Manufacturing

Industry Council (Index)

Once again, Reginald has opened the door for a more expansive discussion around a core business practice. Having studied engineering myself, I understand the reference to thermodynamics but I rarely have never seen it used in this context, well done. This creates a simple dialogue within our businesses that more effectively focuses on the proper separation of running versus reporting.

—Joe Morgan

Founder and CEO

siY, LLC

Former President and Chairman

SONY Chemicals Corporation of America

Former President and CEO, Board Member Standard Register

In this book, Reginald Tomas Lee sheds new light on the traditional way we think about strategic costs.

As companies fiercely compete against each other, solving problems related to cash, profit, and costs demand different innovative thoughts, new ideas, and vision used in synergy with a single objective in mind: Making money.

Reginald introduces the reader to a new and alternative take on cost management, while presenting important operational guidelines for companies that wish to maximize results. He instigates a paradigm shift and presents you with new lenses with which to see how financial performance should be managed.

All of this rather complex content comes in a light, but richly detailed reading.

—Simone Espindola de Oliveira

Manager/Partner of Tecnosul Consulting Cost Engineering,

Blumenau, Santa Catarina, Brazil

Dr. Lee continues his crusade against one of the single most dangerous tools of business: Cost accounting.

Having previously proved that cost accounting is the perfect example of the mantra that there is no right way to do the wrong thing, Strategic Cost Transformation now provides the roadmap for doing all the things cost accounting purports to address—and so spectacularly fails at.

If Alvin Toffler's view that the "illiterate (are) ... those who cannot learn, unlearn, and relearn" is correct, then Lee's latest book should provide the catalyst for literate business owners to finally abandon cost accounting, even if the accounting professionals refuse to.

—Matthew Burgess

Director, View Legal (a timeless law firm)

As a one-time practicing lawyer, I was taught long ago the gospel according to cost accounting. Indeed, cost accounting seemed to the largely innumerate legal profession such a simple, precise, and acceptable doctrine, and formed the bed rock of most professional firms' business model of leveraging people × time × hourly rate. Measurements and rewards of profitability were and still are in most professional firms being made based on cost accounting doctrines. What a shock and relief it was to me to read Dr. Lee's book Lies, Damned Lies and Cost Accounting, which exposed the fraud and the big con that is cost accounting.

Now with Strategic Cost Transformation Dr. Lee not only builds on his expose of cost accounting but also postures a much better, accurate, and effective model to guide the most forward thinking professionals and business owners. Whether the hard core cost accounting aficionados are ever prepared to admit "we were wrong" is another thing entirely.

—John Chisholm

Adjunct Professor, La Trobe Law School

Fellow Elect, College of Law Practice Management

Foreword

Dr. Reginald Tomas Lee begins this book by stating, "We've been fooled. Bamboozled." I have a solemn confession: I was certainly bamboozled. I became a Certified Public Accountant, believing it would allow me to do anything I wanted in the world of commerce since everyone kept telling me it was the language of business. I was taught the importance of proper cost accounting in operating a successful enterprise, from determining a proper price to accurately calculating profit per unit. It was a cohesive body of knowledge, a tangible reality I could grasp, and a prism in which the world of enterprise I so admired could be refracted so as to make sense to a naïve practitioner who believed he knew more than he did.

One of the problems with education is the constant pursuit of practical knowledge at the expense of pursuing answers to profound questions. No doubt we all need practical knowledge to function in everyday life, earn a living, to just get by in the world. But I now realize people are not guided by what they *know*, but rather what they *believe*—their worldview, through which we all refract reality. But what if what you believe isn't true?

This idea was made clear after reading C.S. Lewis's essay, "Transposition," in which he poses the following question: If you live in a two-dimensional landscape painting, how would you respond to someone telling you that the 2D image was just the faintest reflection of a real 3D world? Having grown comfortable in your 2D world—where the angles and edges and math all jibed—you might respond, "Three dimensions? I have no need for that hypothesis."

Strategic Cost Transformation moves you into a 3D world with the concept of Business Domain Management, comprises the Accounting Domain (AD) and the Operations and Cash (OC) Domain. Most businesses focus their attention on the AD, ignoring the more important OC Domain. Understanding the difference between these domains is crucial, and the first step is the unequivocal distinction between a measurement and a metric.

The simple truth is, depending on the cost accounting method used you can calculate radically different cost allocations. Here are just several of the many approved cost accounting methods:

- Standard costing
- Total absorption costing
- Average costing
- Lean costing
- Variable costing
- Marginal costing
- Activity-Based costing

The preceding methods will result in a wide range of cost per unit. This should prove that allocated costs *have nothing to do with cash*.

This is why Reginald argues that cost accounting forces mathematical relationships that don't make sense, and it confuses metrics with measurements. If you walk outside with two thermometers, you will probably get a relatively accurate temperature reading from each. That's a *measurement*. Notice a measurement is not based on a choice.

With cost accounting, however, depending on the method you use, you'll get a wide range of cost per unit—those are *metrics*. This explains the old joke about the accountant who is hired because when asked what 2+2 is, replies, "What would you like it to be?" It is how Enron and Bernie Madoff can report windfall profits, while being cash poor.

Furthermore, Segal's Law applies to cost accounting: "A man with one watch knows what time it is; a man with two watches is never quite sure." Despite these limitations, cost accounting data is treated as gospel. Yet, it is better to be approximately right than precisely wrong. Cost accounting is precisely wrong, and even new methods—such as Activity-Based costing—are just new ways to be wrong.

Reginald's distinction between noncash costs and cash costs is brilliant, not to mention essential for understanding how manipulating costs will not alter cash. The goal is to generate cash profit, not accounting profit. Most costs in organizations today are for capacity: Human capital, facilities, and technology. These costs don't change based on how they are utilized, and yet cost accountants force mathematical relationships that make it appear as if they did, such as cost per hour. The fact is, services and products don't have costs, *organizations* do.

Besides, as Reginald makes clear, "You don't need calculated costs for managerial purposes. The data in the OC Domain are precise and unambiguous [measurements]. The AD information is ambiguous and messy [metrics]. OC Domain provides everything AD does without the drama."

He also points out that "AD creates information that is dangerous to the untrained eye." As a former cost accountant, I can attest that it is just as dangerous to the trained eye, providing a false sense of accuracy and control.

Some examples: Cost accounting can create cash costs by increasing your taxes by misreporting profit; its worldview creates silos—insidiously known as "profit centers"—the equivalent of a wife giving her husband money; it leads to suboptimal pricing, especially if you use cost-plus pricing, since cost per unit changes with volume (and volume depends on price), and cost accounting method used; it leads to misleading Return on Investment analyses, since most investments will not change cash costs; it can lead an organization into having too much capacity as it nonsensically chases economies of scale and lower cost per unit. See General Motors bankruptcy for the perils of this mindset. Reginald instead proposes you model your costs to meet actual demand, not a target cost per unit.

Cost accountants have all sorts of metrics in their toolboxes they claim are the magic bullet for calculating profitability per job, or per product/service. Yet these metrics of margin analysis won't predict the need for additional capacity, or help you model cash flow, nor do they tell you from a pricing perspective if you've left money on the table. Further, these metrics do not help you improve the future performance of your organization. Cost accountants are collectively plunging a ruler into the oven to determine its temperature—it is the wrong tool.

One of Peter's Principles is bureaucracy defends the status quo long past the time when the quo has lost its status. Cost accounting does not deserve to be the apotheosis of pricing, nor organization management. It focuses leaders' limited attention on absolutely the wrong things.

By focusing more on the OC Domain, you will be better able to maximize profitability overall, more aligned with a portfolio approach than a profit per unit approach. But beware: this is not an easy change to make organizationally. The cost accountants and finance types will push back, mightily. Even though they understand cost accounting can be gamed, they will say, "True, but it's better than nothing."

Really? It's as if three friends are lost in New York City, and one happily reports, "Don't worry, I have a map." "But it's a map of Los Angeles," says the second friend, while the third says, "Yes, but it's better than nothing."

In *Strategic Cost Transformation*, Reginald provides us with the correct map: cash flow and capacity modeling. Engineers invented and led us into cost accounting, even though no one paid heed to their warnings that it was a very inexact method. It is only fitting that an engineer now has not only lit a candle in the darkness but is leading us out of a 2D world and back into reality.

Reginald has provided the final nail in the coffin of cost accounting. If you're an educated accountant, you have some *unlearning* to do. But you'll also get exposed to an entirely new dimension of operating your enterprise and be more valuable to it as a result.

—Ronald J. Baker, Radio Talk-Show Host, *The Soul of Enterprise: Business in the Knowledge Economy* (www.thesoulofenterprise.com), Founder of VeraSage Institute, and best-selling author of *Implementing Value Pricing: A Radical Business Model for Professional Firms; Pricing on Purpose: Creating and Capturing Value; Measure What Matters to Customers;* and *Mind Over Matter.*

Preface

Every time I sign a book contract, I believe it will be the last. With *Lies, Damned Lies, and Cost Accounting*, my focus was on showing how and why cost accounting doesn't work the way we believe it does, and why companies should not rely on cost accounting information for managerial purposes. *Lies* had been requested by the founder of the Society of Cost Management, Michael Fournier (may he rest in peace). It was going to be my last book, but as you can see, it was not. In fact, *Project Profitability*, will follow this one by a few months, so I really lied to myself after *Lies*.

When people read *Lies*, it explained a lot of things many figured were wrong. My friend and mentor, Dr. Joe Castellano, a long time accounting professor and all-around good person, told me that the accounting community knew something wasn't right, but they couldn't pinpoint what it was. Sometimes significant breakthroughs come from outside a discipline. Being an engineer, the issues were easier to see. *Lies* highlighted most of these issues. The subsequent question from many readers was, "Ok, so *now* what should we do?"

I thought the answer was to go to my first books. I designed *Lies* to be somewhat of a prequel to *Explicit Cost Dynamics* (ECD) and *Essentials of Capacity Management*. If you want to know what to do, go back to those two books and the answers will be there for you.

There were two problems with the strategy; each book, itself! I believe those books are very content rich, but I'll admit, they are not very well understood. I honestly think the point of *ECD* went over the heads of many who read it, especially cost accounting consultants. Part of this wasn't their fault. It didn't help that it was written as an engineer writes; presumptuous, math focused, and technical. I made the content difficult to access. This wasn't purposeful, I just didn't know how to write. Additionally, it was still assumed by many that all things financial should be considered accounting. This made it hard for some to grasp the notion that there are ways to think about costs that do not follow the rules of accounting, but instead, follow the rules of basic math. People would beat me up because what I was talking about wasn't how accounting worked. I wasn't articulate enough at the time to say, "Of course it doesn't, because it isn't accounting!"

Engineers and many academics did seem to like it, though, as the book was selected as the book of the month by the Institute of Industrial and Systems Engineering (IISE) in January of 2002, and much of the feedback I've gotten from engineers was, "Thank you. This helps us explain how what we do will affect the organization more positively." I still refer back to *ECD* on practically every article and consulting project I'm involved with. It has been the foundation of my work for the past 20 years, both professional and scholarly.

Likewise, *Essentials* wasn't well liked by some in the accounting community. I remember a small-time CPA accounting guy from Florida wrote a scathing review on Amazon, and I'm thinking, "He has no clue what I'm talking about in the sections he's lambasting!" *Essentials*, though, has been a foundational book in organizational capacity management and has been quoted by academics, governments, and professionals because it shapes and defines organizational capacity, the largest expenditure within organizations. It was listed as one of IISE's top books of 2003, and it remains the most cited work I've written.

Both this book and *Lies*, along with the many dozens of articles that I've written since *Essentials* came out, were all strongly tied to those books. The training I've done for companies, the consulting work I've been involved with were all a function of books that accounting people didn't like.

Enter *Strategic Cost Transformation*. Over the past two decades, the ideas have matured and have been tried, tested, validated, and tried again. The concepts in *ECD* and *Essentials* needed to be updated. *Strategic Cost Transformation* takes key elements from the first two books, packages them much more nicely, makes them more easily accessible, and presents them to you for consideration. There are also many new ideas included here that didn't exist when I wrote the first two. Here are a few:

Business Domain Management: breaking companies down into two business domains, the operations and cash or OC Domain, and the Accounting Domain for managerial and analytical purposes. This is a foundational element for cost transformation.

Cash and non-cash costs: One of the most important developments since *Essentials* and *ECD* is the notion that not all costs are cash costs. In fact, most of the costs we think are money, such as the cost for most products, services, and activities are not cash at all.

Input and output capacity: Essentials defined one type of capacity. However, I found that by buying the capacity discussed in *Essentials* (input) you are enabling the ability to create work (output). Both are key to understand, especially when it comes to cost cutting efforts, because what we typically improve is output, yet what we pay for is input. Hence, the improvements do not always lead to improvements in cash.

Isocash curves: I stumbled upon isocash curves. Isocash means equal or same cash, and it demonstrates how business people are often faked into thinking they're doing something positive for the company from a financial perspective when in reality, they aren't. The curves show companies can reduce costs while having zero impact on cash. How does this happen? By reducing non-cash costs. The cash cost, however, remains the same.

Finally, switching gears a bit, I've chosen to use female pronouns solely throughout the book except when referring to specific people. While writing this book, I was deeply affected by the #metoo movement. Mothers, sisters, daughters, and friends of all of us have been exposed to unthinkable situations and acts, and made to think this is, or should be ok or, at a minimum, covered up. Of course, it isn't ok and shouldn't be covered up.

I am blessed to be a product of strong women and of very positive, supporting, and strong men who walked not in front of them, but by their sides along their journeys. The men in my village—my dad, my brother, my godfather, and many others—taught me to be a partner. The women in our village, my mom, my sister, and my godmother especially, taught me, from my earliest memories, the importance of women and how to support and love them. This was one small way I could show support, love, appreciation, and respect for all the women of my village and of the world. Thank you for all you have been, all you are, and all you will be. None of this, or us, would exist without the love, strength, guidance, and wisdom women have and most graciously share.

Acknowledgments

There are several people I'd like to thank for the support they provided me with this project. The first group, of course, is my family. My dad was my #1 hero, and although he was an accountant, I loved him anyway. My mom encouraged me to focus on academic excellence, to never settle, and to push boundaries. If you don't like the content of this book, blame my mom. My sister was always a huge fan and supporter even though she has probably not read a word of my stuff. I still love her anyway! My brother, Marc, is the person to whom I dedicated this book. Marc has been my biggest fan, has read all of the books, has challenged me, encouraged me, and has even traveled internationally to hear me speak. All that, and he's still there whenever I've needed him. He probably should have dropped me after my first book! Seriously, he's my greatest source of inspiration.

Then there's my immediate family. I keep telling my wife Tamara each book is the last, as I'm sure many who've read my stuff secretly wishes for. She doesn't like the writing process but has supported me as I disappear and do all the things she told me she doesn't like me doing when I write books. The kids have been amazing. Ashton, Isabella, Sophia, and Rey (Jr) have been amazingly giving and supportive. I'd like to think they have selflessly given their time and passed on experiences to help make this book a reality, but they may also like the fact that I'm not all up in their business because I have writing to do. And then, there's Erin.

Erin is my first child. She has been a supporter for each and every one of my books, and most of all, she's a valued friend. I'm blessed by the notion that she is an integral part of the writing process, now. From editing the content and challenging me on ideas, to telling me sometimes how badly my writing sucks, her assessments are sometimes harsh, but always true. Few things make me prouder than her helping me with this process.

I'd also like to thank a number professional and personal friends. First, Dr. Glen Johnson, my PhD committee chair has been a long-time friend and advocate. More importantly, he supported my desires to study business as an engineering student. Scott Isenberg and Dr. Ken Merchant placed their faith and trust in me to write another book for Business Expert Press. I'm grateful and hope this book doesn't cause them to disown me. Ron Baker has challenged me to get this book out yesterday. His support and contributions to both the concepts in this book and the motivation to finish and share the ideas have been greatly appreciated. Dr. Joe Castellano, too, has been a mentor, supporter, and friend. Joe's wisdom and knowledge have deeply shaped me and my content. Sergio Gonzales has become a friend and I've appreciated our times together and our conversations, both in and outside of México on these topics. Dr. Luis Hernandez has been instrumental making sure I was in México training companies on these topics through Index México, the Mexican association of maquiladoras. Finally, thank you to Maria Gonzales for coordinating my involvement with Angok, and bringing the concepts in this book to faculty and business professionals in México. Finally, I'd like to thank my friend Ross Shahandeh has also made a valuable contribution to this, and my next project. I'm grateful for his support.

Lastly, as always, I want to thank Rob and Tony from Four80East. I continue to be inspired by their work. Thanks, guys. To close, I'd like to thank my friends Pepe and Pedro, for being there when I was struggling for ideas and words. I appreciate you all.

Introduction

Strategic Cost Transformation is about transforming how we think about and manage costs. We tend to think about costs as accounting values. We think about costs as being money, and that if we reduce costs, we save money. We believe we should look to cost data for answers and guidance on improving financial performance.

This book proposes all three of these notions are incorrect. Costs as cash are not accounting values at all. In fact, all cash costs occur independently of accounting. Accounting costs are derived, to a certain extent, from cash costs, but are generally not cash themselves. When you think about the cost to perform an activity such as to process an invoice or to answer a phone, do you pay the calculated cost amount to someone every time the activity is performed? Or products, when you produce the n+1st item, to whom are you paying the $2.63 you say it costs you to make the item? Finally, looking to accounting to guide you for managerial purposes is a very dangerous practice. Some have likened managing using accounting data to driving by looking in the rearview mirror. However, this description is not accurate. Looking in the rearview mirror to see where you are going supposes the information in the rearview mirror can tell you something about where you've been. What if it doesn't? What if it can't?

The mirror, in this case, is accounting information which, we will see, is one of practically an infinite number of possible descriptions of the reality a company has experienced. Reading this book, you will find the descriptions that are created by accounting information can be highly distorted. Additionally, when you consider an activity that costs $3.25 to perform, what do you know from that value? What was the salary of the person who performed the activity (cash)? How efficiently did they perform the task? How much output did they create? What was the demand for the output? Do we know if we produced too many or not enough? What else did they do? We have insight into none of the information about how we got there. A more accurate description might be that one is not looking into a mirror, but instead, a backward-facing kaleidoscope; a distorted representation of the past that provides little to no insight into what you're looking at and, hence, it will fail at telling you where you need to go.

This book is broken down into three parts to help shape a transformation of cost modeling and analysis from being accounting and non-cash focused to being corporate-wide and cash focused. Part I, The Issue, creates a foundation for the challenges companies face, the limitations of the tools they're using, and a reason for action. If your firm's goal or objective is to make money, accounting information is not a sufficient enough tool to help the leaders make decisions. There needs to be something that is bigger, more comprehensive, and more mathematically accurate. Enter Business Domain Management (BDM).

Part II focuses on the concept of BDM. Within BDM, organizations are broken down into two business domains: the Operations and Cash (OC) Domain and the Accounting Domain. The OC Domain is where business transactions occur, work is performed, output is created, and sold when possible. All business activities, what was bought, consumed, and sold, happen in the OC Domain. Key to the OC Domain is capacity. Capacity is what you buy in anticipation of use or demand. In this context, capacity is both pervasive within organizations and is their largest expense. As such, it is where cash modeling begins. A good portion of Part II focuses on the operating and cash dynamics of capacity.

The second is the Accounting Domain. I argue the Accounting Domain is for reporting what happened in the OC Domain based on the rules of accounting, scope chosen, and accounting techniques used. It is not an actual representation of what happened. Instead, it is a transformed image based on assumptions and often contrived relationships that create a non-unique solution. It is not unique because, as I will explain, the assumptions and relationships describing what happened in the OC Domain can change, giving different solutions even though nothing changes in the OC Domain. I discuss the transformation process that converts OC Domain data into accounting information in the Accounting Domain.

In Part III, I focus on the execution of the transformation process. Now that we understand where cash data come from, the role capacity plays, and the transformation of operations and cash data into Accounting

Domain information, the question is, "How do you manage in the new environment?" I begin with how to model money and project cash. There will also be the inevitable conflicts between the two domains. In many scenarios, data may suggest that improvements in OC Domain cash may have a negative effect on Accounting Domain profit. In other scenarios, improvements to accounting profit will have a negative effect on cash. I follow this with a discussion how to model the cash impact of improvement projects using these techniques, and close with factors to consider while budgeting.

I hope this book is insightful and valuable. My wife would kill me if I took all this time away from the family to put out a product that is useless, especially since I told her my last book was going to be my last book.

Thank you for taking the time to consider these ideas. One of the most valuable gifts is time. Thank you for your gift to me.

PART I

The Issue

CHAPTER 1

Bamboozled by Numbers

We've been fooled. Bamboozled. What has fooled you, me, and practically every business person on the planet? Accounting information. It is pervasive and practically everyone uses it. Kids with neighborhood lemonade stands calculate how much money they believe each cup of lemonade will make. Executives at major global companies look at accounting information as they try to "make more money" by increasing profits. Hospital executives try to reduce the length and, therefore, the cost of a patient's stay in the hospital to improve profitability. Those who offer capital and debt services look at accounting information to determine whether, and to what extent, the companies they are looking at funding are making money.

See a common thread? People look at accounting information such as costs and profitability to determine whether a company is making money, and for guidance and information about how to make more. We are led to believe this accounting information represents money and making money, but it doesn't provide us with the information we truly need to make money, and I'm not convinced it even tries. For example, if accounting were about money, why are there noncash items on the income statement where profit is calculated? Why can the value of an asset on the balance sheet be determined by subjective data and arbitrary relationships? Why, when using the indirect method to create a cash flow statement, can you use net income data from the income statement when the net income calculations include data from accruals and the cost of goods sold (COGS)? Why is this a problem, you ask?

In my last book, *Lies, Damned Lies, and Cost Accounting*, I argued extensively, and will again here, that COGS, the key cost component for gross margins, isn't money. It has the same unit of measure as money; dollars for instance, but COGS is an opinion of worth or value. It is not money. Therefore, the gross margin calculation, itself, is questionable from a cash perspective. How can you take revenue, which, let's say for now is money, and subtract something that isn't money from it? But revenue doesn't get a free pass either. You can recognize revenue for a sale before you have received money from the sale. In other words, you can calculate a profit from revenue you haven't received. If that's true, the revenue used in profit calculations isn't always money either. This leaves us with a calculation that is supposed to be about money, but instead often compares money not received to an opinion of value from money spent in a previous period. Somehow, this is supposed to tell us whether we've made money in the current period.

The idea of tying COGS to revenue from a sale is an accrual technique called matching. Here is how absurd matching is. Let's add a bit of detail to the earlier example. Say I sell you a coffee cup for $5 in February. I made it last year in December and my COGS was calculated to be $2.50. Matching basically says, "take that $2.50 and tie it to revenue from the product when it is sold." In other words, I incur the $2.50 cost from a profit perspective in February when I sell you the cup and recognize the revenue. I sell you something in February, but I incurred the cash cost of buying labor and materials months before. To make it even more fun, I let you pay me in March. I can calculate the profit in February by taking revenue I won't receive until March and subtract a noncash value based on production activities—money spent from two months ago—and calculate a value I think is money. How much sense does that make if the objective is to understand whether you are making money in the current period?

The reliance on accounting information has caused really smart people to do not-so-smart things. For example, consider make-versus-buy decisions where a company has to decide whether they are going to make a product or buy an equivalent from another company. An accountant calculates an internal cost of $3.18 for an item her company makes. An outside provider will sell an equivalent to her company for $3.05. She believes she is saving 13¢ per unit by going with the outsourced option. However, there are two problems. First, the $3.18 is a cost calculated using a particular scope and allocation methodology. If she changed scope or costing methodology from standard costing to activity-based costing, for instance, she will more than likely come up with a different cost.

The calculated cost could just as easily be $3.25 or $2.91. In fact, the numbers can differ sometimes by as much as 200 percent.[1]

Second, whatever number she calculates is not cash anyway. A calculated cost is an opinion of the value of resources or capacity consumed in making a product or performing a task. Say you perform a task at work that takes ten minutes. Someone calculated that task to cost $25. When you perform that task, no money changes hands; there is no cash transaction. How did the $25 come about? Someone likely put a rate on time, such as $2.50 per minute, hence, a 10-minute task would *cost* $25. As we will find later, that number will change based on the assumptions that go into the $2.50 per minute calculation. When doing the make-versus-buy savings analysis, our accountant compared an opinion of value that isn't money and whose magnitude can change by tweaking a few assumptions or parameters (make) to spending money (buy). Then, she pats herself on the back when it appears as though she's saved 13¢ even though that number could just as easily be 20¢ or −14¢, and, again, it isn't money anyway. Imagine how many jobs have been lost as a result of analyses such as these that are mathematically unsound.

I don't blame accounting. Accounting is like a butter knife. Butter knives were designed to cut butter. Once we try to use the butter knife to cut things it wasn't designed to cut, or use it to do things it wasn't designed to do, it fails. Butter knives are not good at cutting leather, or cutting down trees, and they're horrible hammers. Knocking the butter knife because it can't cut down trees or drive nails is senseless. Because it's good at cutting one thing doesn't mean it is ok to extrapolate that into all things cutting, or to use it in any other type of situation you can conceive.

Accounting was arguably designed to report. Because accounting creates a portion of a company's financial information (cutting butter) doesn't mean it should be used for all others matters that appear to be money related (cutting down trees). It is the overly ambitions academics, consultants, and business folks who look at cost accounting and say, "Hey, we can calculate a cost for this pencil (cutting butter). What if

---

[1] Cooper, R., and R.S. Kaplan. September–October 1988. *Measure Costs Right: Make the Right Decisions*, 100. Harvard Business Review.

we use the same basic approach to calculate the cost of an activity such as processing an invoice (cutting leather)? How cool is that?" Or, "We calculate profits for reporting purposes (butter), why don't we calculate profits for customers, or departments, or patients (cutting down trees)? How cool is that?" It isn't.

Since accounting techniques were designed for reporting, certain concessions were necessary for it to perform properly. Let's consider the early textiles companies. Around 1812, the textiles industry began to integrate vertically. This created a challenge. Before, companies would buy output from artisans. There was a clear transaction—money for a rug, for instance. Companies started hiring artisans and paying them a wage. Let's say this wage was $2 per day. This creates a challenge when reporting profit. It was easy before. They bought a rug for $1, so that was the cost. Now, they're buying the artisan's time. Whether they made no rugs or an infinite amount in one day, the cash cost for labor was still $2. The question is, if you have to report the gross margins, revenue – COGS, how do you determine the cost of a rug? This is a question accounting is still trying to answer 200 plus years later. It's an extremely challenging mathematical question, and every new cost accounting technique tries to come up with a better way answer it.

The issue lies in what accounting is asking math to do. There is no mathematical relationship between the $2 you pay an artisan worker for a day of her time and the rugs she makes during that time. But if you're required to report the cost of the rug, you will need a relationship to calculate it. The problem is, a relationship doesn't exist. Since it doesn't exist, you have to make one up, and since it is made up, it is arbitrary. This calculation is a questionable move mathematically when used for reporting, so in the context of creating managerial information, it can be downright dangerous.

The result has been a misunderstanding of what accounting information tells us, when to use it, and how it's different from making money. Consider these four, very common cost-related sacred cows:

1. Costs are money
2. Reducing costs saves money

3. More profit equals more money

4. Costs and profit are measured

Each one of these is false, but we've been bamboozled into thinking they're true. Let's consider each in turn.

Costs Are Money

Say you make $60,000 per year and you perform a two-hour activity. Someone asks, "What did that activity cost?" How would you figure it out? One way may be to try to turn your salary into an hourly wage, such as $31 for each hour you work, but how? Do you assume a 2000-hour work year? 2040? 1960? What number do you use? It's a guess, at best, in foresight. You won't know how many hours you worked until the year is over, and even then, do you consider only productive work time? Are breaks included? There is a lot of subjectivity just in calculating an hourly rate.

Let's say you use 2,000 hours for simplicity to calculate an hourly wage of $30. The task takes two hours, so you decide the activity costs $60. There are two problems with this. First, the $30 per hour is not an hourly wage. It's a proxy. You aren't paid by the hour. If an hourly worker works another hour, the company pays her another $30. If you work another hour and you're salaried, you're late for dinner and you are going home with no extra money. As a result, the $30 and, therefore, the $60 cost for the activity are not cash. It's *one of many possible* representations of the value of your time. Second, to reinforce this notion, if the $60 were cash, who is your company paying when you perform the activity? Does your company lose $60 when you perform the task or save $60 if you don't? No. There is no cash transaction when you perform the activity, so the $60 is not money.

I call these calculated costs $cost_{NON-CASH}$ or $cost_{NC}$, so people know they aren't cash values. The only cash value in this scenario is what you're paid in salary, which is $5,000 per month before taxes. The cash cost for you to work for the company, paid as your salary, is designated $cost_C$ for $cost_{CASH}$. Although they're both *costs* and they have the same unit name, dollars, they are very different. One is money and the other is not, suggesting only some costs are money.

Reducing Costs = Saving Money

Let's say your company spends tens of millions of dollars buying an ERP system for a huge transformation and hires a very large global consulting firm with tons of consultants to implement it. One of the thousands of value opportunities they've included in their business case to help them justify you paying all that money, is the $60, two-hour task that you perform. They propose their new software will cut the amount of time it takes you to perform the task in half, from two hours to one. This would suggest a reduction in cost from $60 to $30. Let's say this task is performed by you and others in your organization 1000 times per day. The consultants will claim to save your company $30,000 per day. Over the course of a 52-week year, this equates to $7.8M. Wow. Impressive, right? No.

First, remember the subjectivity that went into figuring out $60 in the first place. Next, recall the $60 was not cash. Finally, you all aren't being paid any less money as a result of spending less time doing the task. All the solution did was reduce the amount of your time that is consumed performing the task. This, of course, leads to a lower calculated cost, or $cost_{NC}$, but you are still paid the same and you still have other work to do. The key difference is, now you will have more time to do it. Overall, no money has been saved. Imagine the poor soul who agreed to $23M in savings over three years and bought the software and expensive consulting, believing they will see savings for the firm. Large $cost_{NC}$ savings may occur, but no money is being saved.

More Profit = More Money

Assume every time you perform the $60 task, you're able to charge a customer $100 for the service. After the improvement, there is no increase in demand for the task, so you will not be performing the task more than before. Your technology solution has now reduced your cost, $cost_{NC}$, from

$60 to $30. Does that mean you've now made $70 as a company versus $40 before? If so, where is the additional money coming from? They still pay you $60,000 regardless of how much time it takes. The company still receives $100 in revenue each time you perform the task. From a cash perspective, cost$_C$ is constant, hence, you have not made any more money. From an accounting perspective you have improved margins. Cash says no more money has been made and accounting says profit has increased. That's a problem.

Now, you may try to argue the efficiency improvement may improve the cash position because the company can sell more or reduce capacity by reducing the number of people employed. In other words, the efficiency enhancements *caused* other improvements to occur. This is like blaming airplane crashes on gravity. Gravity does not cause a plane to crash. It is an enabler. If there is a significant enough failure, the plane will fall. Similarly, efficiency improvements don't automatically create savings, they enable them. If there is a significant enough improvement, you can make changes. If you have more time, you can perform the task more frequently potentially creating more output. The financial improvement from increased output, when the output is salable, comes from greater revenues, not reduced costs. There is a caveat, though. There's an assumption there is demand for the output. What if there isn't?

The only cost cutting opportunity, in this case, is reducing capacity; buying fewer or cheaper people. There must be a managerial decision and act to change the staff level. The IT solution improvement won't fire people and people won't fire themselves. Although the people are more efficient, something must occur to realize cash savings.

This notion is often overlooked by managers willing to "do good." I was once brought into a situation where a major global technology firm needed to reduce costs significantly. The leadership needed eight figure reductions in costs, but they weren't willing to part with people. They believed by making their people more efficient, $20+ million dollars would just disappear. Unfortunately, money doesn't work that way, even though scores of consultants make such promises. As long as the people were still on their payroll, the cash costs would still remain, hampering their ability to realize the desired savings.

Costs and Profit Are Measured

I often see consultants telling prospects they measure costs and profit. I hear and read academics talking about the notion of measuring costs. Robin Cooper and Robert Kaplan, Harvard Business School professors even wrote an article for the Harvard Business Review titled *Measure Costs Right: Make the Right Decisions*. If anyone tells you they measure costs and profits, and they use accounting techniques to do so, you should look at them funny. Measures suggest certainty. You can measure by counting and you can measure using a measuring device or standard such as a tape measure or a thermometer. In each case, within the precision of the tool or approach, you'll converge on the same answer. It's 55 degrees F plus or minus 2 degrees. Twenty-three people walked in the front door. Cash is a measured value. You know you spent $5,000 or received $2,718.35. These amounts are known, or at least should be. If they aren't, that's a topic for another book.

Accounting costs and profit are just the opposite. We didn't measure the $60 for each two-hour task, we figured it out; we calculated it. We made assumptions to create a rate of $30 per hour, which could have just as easily been $20 or $40 depending on the assumptions we made, scope we used, and costing technique we chose. How realistic would it be if you walked outside to check the temperature and found it's either 55 degrees, 72 degrees, or 12 degrees? Or if either 12, 17, or 33 people walked through the door? How much sense does this make when you're looking for a precise, measured value such as what something costs? None.

Accounting costs, therefore, aren't measured. They're calculated. Profit, too, is calculated. You don't measure either, you figure them out, and a different set of assumptions will lead to a different cost or profit. If you have multiple costs and profit values, which one is right? Taking liberties with Segal's Law, *a woman with a watch knows what time it is. A woman with two watches is never quite sure.* This is practically the opposite of measuring something where your opinions and ideas don't matter and will not, therefore, change the outcome. Neither the temperature nor the actual number of people who walk through a door are affected by your opinion of what they should be. However, with calculated costs you can use practically any assumptions and techniques you want. Want to reduce taxes? Make profit smaller by considering more factors that will increase your costs. Want to improve market value or improve credit worthiness? Accounting can accommodate. This is not accounting's fault. It is how we have chosen to exploit the tool.

What's sad is, this information seems almost like a drug of choice to business leaders. There is an addiction to it and a fear of discontinuing its use, even when they know the information is either suspect or downright wrong. Many who have read, *The Goal* by Eli Goldratt, for instance, loved what he had to say. They buy into Dr. Goldratt's ideas, talk about how great the book is, and then turn around and ignore what he said and focus, instead, on the cost accounting numbers he lambasts. Others, too, have questioned the relevance of cost accounting information. Taiichi Ohno, the leader within Toyota who was responsible for the Toyota Production System, the precursor to lean, was adamant about not using cost accounting. In fact, Ohno reportedly suggested, it wasn't enough to drive cost accountants out of his factory. He had to drive cost accounting out of the heads of his people. He knew the potential negative effects of cost accounting information, yet many companies I've worked with who claim to have implemented lean still use cost accounting information. Dr. H. Thomas Johnson, coauthor of *Relevance Lost* with Dr. Robert Kaplan of activity-based costing fame realized, after *Relevance Lost* was published, that they were wrong and spent years trying to address the issue, writing books such as *Relevance Regained* and *Profit Beyond Measure*. The information is out there, but we refuse to use it.

There are options that can allow for a shift away from misused and misunderstood accounting information toward an environment that is more effective at modeling whether you made money and provides better context for managerial decisions. It all begins with The Goal.

CHAPTER 2

The Goal-Making Money

One of my favorite business books is *The Goal* written by Dr. Eliyahu "Eli" Goldratt. In the book, Dr. Goldratt makes a point I, and many others, have found to be powerful in terms of its ability to rally company employees around an idea and focus organizational efforts. He proposed the goal of a company is to make money, a simple notion. Of course, as usually happens, many business intellectuals tried to argue that making money was an objective or something other than the goal. The goal might be to make products for the greater good, or to make technologically sound products, or to offer services to address a key need in a target population.

These may be ideas the company's founder sought to achieve when she started the company. The company's leadership may have decided to target these ideas in their strategic plan. However, none of this can be accomplished without making money. Money is lifeblood. It provides energy. Without it, companies fail to thrive and, in fact, survive. The goal in managing and running the company should be to make money doing what the company was created to do.

It's pretty clear, given the importance of money, we need the right tools to guide us and help us understand how to make it, to assess if we have made it, and to determine how much we have made. This, in turn, will help us understand the extent to which we are, or are not, achieving The Goal.

As suggested in the last chapter, companies use accounting for money-related information. They look to understand and manage costs with the objective of being more profitable; to make more money. The question, however, is whether accounting, specifically cost accounting, has the ability to provide us with the information that tells us whether we are making money and how to make more. The simple answer and the basis of much of this book is, "no." In fact, focusing on calculated costs along with cost accounting and profit information are almost the worst tools you could use by themselves. Any tool that tells you by improving a particular metric you can become more profitable when, in fact, it causes you to lose money, should be considered useless. This would be like driving and having your GPS tells you to speed up when you're at a red light. This can happen when focusing solely on accounting information. Again, this is not accounting's fault. It is being asked to do something it was not designed to do.

This creates dangerous and unpredictable situations and management decisions. Here are just two examples. The first was a client looking to improve it gross margins through productivity enhancements. Simplifying the situation to make the point, assume a laborer is the only cost and she makes $30 per hour. On average, she makes 15 widgets per hour. By increasing her efficiency, she can now produce 20 versus 15 widgets in an hour. The cost per widget goes down, leading to the perception that the company is making more money on each widget assuming the sales price remains the same.

The reality is quite different. The sales price did remain the same and what she was paid on an hourly basis didn't change. However, the "cost per unit" (cost$_{NC}$) was lower, leading to a higher gross margin and, therefore, a higher taxable income. Revenue was the same, money paid in salary was the same, and taxes increased, so the company made less money. Now, consider this as another potentially dangerous situation. What if the company believes they can reduce price as a result of the lower cost? The amount going out in labor is the same as it was initially, and the amount of money coming in is less.

The second example is a client that had desirable gross margins that may have been putting them out of business. Let's say they bought material processed a particular way for an accounting cost of $1 per unit; they would buy 10,000 units for $10,000. If their products sold for $10, they had a gross margin of $9, again, simplifying to get the point across. Our suggestion was that they buy materials using another technology, which was assumed to be more expensive, to save money. Their counter, of course, was that they would lose money with the proposed technology. I asked how much it would cost to buy 5,000 units. They responded, "$8,000." I replied, "Yes, you're losing money, alright!" "How? If we bought the more expensive product, our gross margins would go from $9

($10 − $1) to $8.40 ($10 − $1.60)!" Then, I asked, "How much demand is there for the product, on average?" Around 5,000 per SKU. "So, you generate $50,000 in revenue?" "Yes." "Would you rather spend $10,000 to make $50,000 or $8,000 to make $50,000?"

Remember, the accounting profit calculation is not money. While their interpretation of the situation given the math they used was right, the math they used was wrong.

In these cases, the desired answer for the companies, from their perspective, involved looking at cost accounting information. Ultimately, however, they found it wasn't the right answer when it came to making money. In fact, I'd argue cost accounting information, alone, does not provide anywhere near enough relevant information about cash costs to allow for maximum cash flow. There are a few reasons for this.

Let's think about accounting costs. Accounting costs are calculated values. Someone has to figure out what the product, service, or activity costs, so they are $cost_{NC}$. To figure out a cost, there are several ways to do so based on what is being emphasized, what data are used, how the data are used, and ease of maintenance or use. That's one opinion why you have so many different approaches to calculating costs. Each technique focuses on a different way to calculate a cost. Standard costing emphasizes standards, average costing is about ease and equal distributions of allocated costs, not accuracy, and activity based is tied to drivers with the objective being more accurate allocations.

In the end, however, the sole purpose of these methods is to calculate costs. *They are all notionally the same.* Each one attempts to solve the same problem: "What does this product, service, activity, or outcome cost?" Each method therefore, has its own approach or philosophy regarding how to calculate this cost. Each, then, will calculate different answers. Here's a question to consider. If these calculated costs were money, how, logically, can the amount of money you spent, a tangible and measured value, change based on the technique you've chosen to use to calculate it? If I buy something for $1 and sell it for $2, I made $1 regardless of anyone's opinion, cost allocations, or any other factors.

This is similar to the observer effect in physics. The suggestion in physics is that when we observe certain phenomena, the observation process changes what we are observing. If we use light to observe the location of an electron, the light will move the electron to a different position. This would be like GPS satellites moving your car every time they try to understand your position. Similarly, our costing techniques change the calculated cost, suggesting you will not converge, mathematically, on one cost. Instead, you will diverge to many costs.

Another factor to consider is scope; what should be included and left out of the cost calculation? With product costs, for instance, how is overhead handled? What should and should not be included? Who should be included? If you're a hospital calculating the cost of a patient stay, do you include the folks who move patients around from room to room? Billing? If you're in manufacturing, should defects be included? You'll get a different answer if you spread costs across 100 good units versus 100 good and 10 bad units. What about warehousing and shipping? Are they in or out of product costs? In my previous experience helping companies with the design, development, and implementation of cost management systems, these and similar questions are often harder to answer and agree to than the allocation method. Because they're up for debate, the choices made are subjective. Because they're subjective and they influence the value of the calculated cost, the calculated cost, itself, is subjective. As with any analysis, your answer is limited by the least precise part of your model. If you're guessing whether to include warehouse costs in your product costs, for instance, what difference does $0.001 matter at an operation? Get rid of warehouse costs and you might change the product cost by $1.00. As with costing methodologies, decisions you make based on subjective ideas should not and cannot change how much money you spent.

The last factor to consider is how certain accounting principles violate a basic rule regarding the timing of cash flow. Consider this. Say it's March 1. You want to know how much money you made in the month of February, and how much you had at the end of the month. How would you figure it out? You start by considering how much money you had at the beginning of February. Let's say, on February 1, you had $100. Then, you would consider the money that came in through the month, say $50, the money you spent ,assume $30. You end up making $20. Straightforward, right? This is summarized in Equation 2.1. You ended February with $120. The key factors for consideration were the time period (one month), what you started with ($100), what you received ($50) and what you spent, and therefore no longer have ($30).

$$Cash_{FINAL} = Cash_{INITIAL} + \Sigma Cash_{IN} - \Sigma Cash_{OUT} \qquad (2.1)$$

Let's go back to the scenario in Chapter 1 and matching. What we didn't consider, and what matching allows is money you spent December or expect in March. However, this is exactly what happens with matching. Revisiting, calculated accounting costs are tied to opinions about what factors should be considered in and out of scope when calculating costs. They're based on opinions about the technique that should be used to allocate costs. They may be considered from timeframes outside the one being considered. In that context, how can accounting costs represent money? They can't.

Now let's consider profit. The basic equation for profit is:

$$Profit = Revenues - Costs \qquad (2.2)$$

This relationship is simple enough, until you factor in the issues I mentioned previously with cost types and matching. Some are not money and matching considers costs we spent previously and may receive after the analysis period. The profit equation then becomes something like this:

$$Profit = \Sigma\, Revenues_{RECOGNIZED} - \Sigma\, Costs_{MATCHED} - \Sigma\, Costs_{C\text{-}RECOGNIZED}$$
$$_{IN\ PERIOD} - \Sigma\, Cost_{NC\text{-}RECOGNIZED\ IN\ PERIOD}$$

Where

$Revenue_{RECOGNIZED}$ is the revenue recognized in the period by accounting
$Costs_{MATCHED}$ are the costs associated with the sales recognized in the period
$Costs_{C\text{-}RECOGNIZED\ IN\ PERIOD}$ are the cash costs such as cash sales, general, and administrative (SG&A) costs recognized in the period
$Cost_{NC\text{-}RECOGNIZED\ IN\ PERIOD}$ are non-cash costs such as depreciation and amortization that are recognized in the period

This is clearly nonsensical, crossing timelines and even value types.

The other factor to consider is basic arithmetic. Let's say you did receive cash in February. I proposed last chapter accounting costs were not actually money. If this is the case, how do you subtract costs, which aren't money, from money? We can't subtract pickup trucks from trees, and have the answer be trees. We learned in second grade we can't subtract dissimilar things such as apples from oranges, houses from jars of pickles, or pickup trucks from trees, right? Yet that's what is happening when we try to subtract an opinion from money. Second, recall, each costing approach/scope scenario gives you a different cost, which will lead to different profit. Therefore, your profit is significantly influenced by your choices of how to calculate costs and the data you include in the calculation. Consider this. In our February cash example, it was clear how much money we made. From an accounting perspective, we can actually change what we think we made in profit based on the scope we choose and the techniques we use to calculate costs. Again, how can a choice we make determine how much money we made? We can make $10 using one approach or $20 using another? How can this make sense if we are focused on cash and the cash transactions are unaffected by accounting technique? Money is a measure and it is absolute. Profit, however, is a metric that can be influenced.

If the goal is to make money, and if accounting doesn't serve this purpose, what should we do instead? I'd like to propose that there be a strategic cost transformation from accounting analyses to a more holistic framework called business domain management, or BDM. BDM looks at the business comprehensively and is designed to model cash and capacity, support the use of accounting for reporting purposes, and enable alignment between accounting/finance and operations. This transformation of costs to a larger and more comprehensive framework will focus on the factors that affect cash, provide a comprehensive look at business operations and cash, and form a foundation from which accounting information is determined. From this, more effective cash-based decisions can be made. This is the subject for the next chapter.

CHAPTER 3

Strategic Cost Transformation—An Overview

What Is Strategic Cost Transformation?

Strategic cost transformation (SCT), here, is about transforming the scope and focus of cost analysis from traditional accounting-based cost management systems to a corporate wide system that models and aligns cash, operations, and accounting. This system, Business Domain Management (BDM), includes and models each of two business domains; the Accounting Domain and the Operations and Cash Domain (OC Domain). Traditional accounting information such as calculated costs and profit reside in the Accounting Domain.

We typically look to the Accounting Domain to provide information that will help us make cost management decisions. However, as mentioned last chapter, our companies need cash to sustain themselves. Cash, and calculated costs and profit, are very different.[1] Cash is money, a measure, and money is exact. Calculated costs and profit are reporting metrics that can be influenced by opinion and arbitrary assumptions. To improve cash, you must understand it through effective cash modeling. Effective cash models capture the factors that affect cash dynamics. This happens in the OC Domain. A complete picture of your organization and its operational and financial performance cannot exist without modeling the OC Domain. BDM, combines the Accounting Domain and the OC Domain into one framework that provides a comprehensive view of all operations, cash, and accounting information (Exhibit 3.1).

---

[1] Lee, R.T. March-April 2016. "Why Profit Doesn't Translate into Cash." *Journal of Corporate Accounting & Finance* 27, no. 3, pp. 63–66.

Capacity, cash flow and business activities   Calculated financial information

Exhibit 3.1 If the Accounting Domain is one dimension, the OC Domain is the second. Having a 2-D view of your organization will create greater clarity regarding what is happening in the organization, why, and what you can do to improve than a 1-D view can offer. This is the foundation of Business Domain Management, which is the objective of SCT

Inset: Artificial Cost Reductions

One challenge of working with calculated costs in the Accounting Domain is the opportunity to create artificial cost savings. There are two ways by which costs are typically proposed to be reduced. The first is to increase output at a given input level; increase the number of widgets made or customer service calls answered by the same people. The other way is to consume less capacity to create the same output; reduce the time to make each widget or to answer each call. In both the cases, $cost_{NC}$ is reduced while $cost_C$ remains the same.

Increased Output

Consider the output of someone being paid $30 per hour. Dividing the wage by output creates the average cost curve in Exhibit A. This is also an isocash or equal cash curve, as the cash spent on labor does not change. Notice, by going from point A to point B on the curve, there is a cost reduction involved; from $7.50 to $3.75. However, the cash spent is still the same. This suggests there could be a cost reduction in the Accounting Domain that will not be reflected in cash.

Another situation to consider is one found in Exhibit B. Exhibit B shows two isocash curves:, one for $30 and the other for $20. With the

$20 isocash curve, it is clear you would be spending less money for the hour of work. However, this chart shows the cost per unit output is lower at B ($3.75) than it is at A' ($5). This may cause one to think they are better off spending $30 and increasing their output than by moving to a cheaper, lower, isocash curve ($20). Not understanding this will often cause overspending and maintaining higher capacity cash costs in the name of improving profit.

Reduced Consumption

Consider the same $30 and a task that takes 10 minutes. Exhibit C suggests by reducing the time to eight minutes, the cost will go down. However, you're still on the same isocash curve, so money is not saved. As was suggested earlier, to reduce cash costs, you will have to move from point A to a position on a lower isocash curve, such as point A'. Exhibit D suggests cash savings only happen when you shift to a lower isocash curve, regardless of whether time has been taken out of the activity.

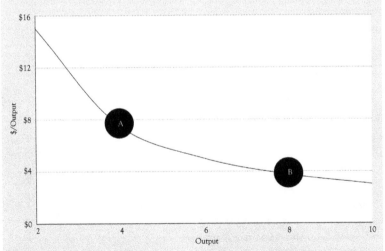

Exhibit A Isocash output curve for $30 per hour. Going from A to B involves accounting cost savings not cash savings

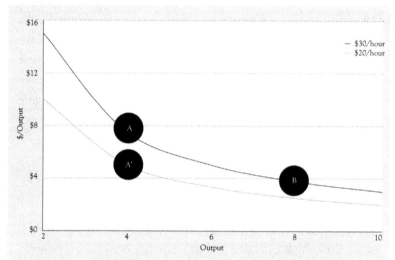

Exhibit B *Two isocash output curves, $30 and $20. Only when moving to another, lower isocash curve, such as moving from A to A', will you reduce cash costs*

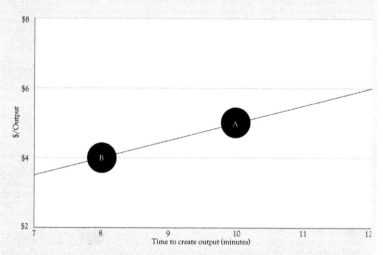

Exhibit C *Isocash capacity consumption curve. Although less capacity is consumed by reducing the time to create output, you're still on the same isocash curve*

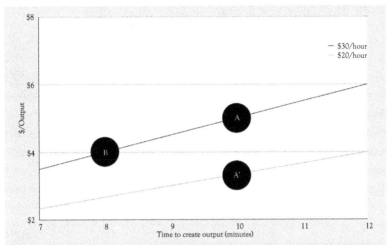

Exhibit D *Two isocash consumption curves $30 and $20. Only by moving to a lower isocash curve will money be saved*

Why Is a Transformation Necessary?

To stay in business, companies must make money. We look at gross and contribution margins, for instance, to understand whether a particular product, service, or opportunity has made money. We look at cost information to identify targets for cost reduction. However, since accounting information does not represent money, cash, it is limited in its ability to model cash. This suggests it's limited in its ability to tell you whether you've made cash and why. It cannot offer precise information that guides you how to reduce cash costs. It cannot provide data regarding what specific managerial actions can lead to making more money. In fact, the modeling can be so inaccurate, there are situations where cost accounting may show a $cost_{NC}$ reduction when, in fact, the situation would increase $cost_C$ (see Inset: Artificial Cost Reductions).

If managing and reducing costs to make more money is the objective, cost accounting tools aren't enough. The Accounting Domain and cost accounting offer a one dimensional (1-D) look at your business, but business exists in what is akin to a two-dimensional world (2-D). 1-D analyses are incapable of fully comprehending things that exist in a 2-D world. The information from the second dimension has to be reduced, simplified, or even eliminated. Consider, for example, the cost of a product. You calculate an electric pencil/stylus costs your company $19.38 to produce. What does that number tell you about the size of your organization, your cash requirements, how efficiently you're operating, how much output you created, what output you created, or how it was made? Nothing. It only offers a very limited representation of the activities that happened previously. To understand what happened comprehensively, you need another dimension, one that includes the business activities and cash transactions that are ultimately used to calculate the $19.38.

The objective of SCT isn't to change accounting by creating a new costing approach or allocation schema. There are already enough of those out there. Instead, the purpose is to expand the narrative by offering a different, accretive, dimension of data and information. It starts by using the OC Domain to create a second dimension to your accounting analyses. The OC Domain adds a more complete perspective of business performance. For instance, the OC Domain answers questions such as:

- How much are you spending on capacity?
- How much capacity do you have?
- How efficiently, effectively, and productively is it being consumed?
- What is consuming it?
- What work/output is being created?
- How does the output align with demand for it?
- Are you generating cash from the output?
- What products, services, and consumers consume capacity at greater or lesser rates?
- How do we project cash?

The answers to these questions, the operations and cash data and the resulting information, are often used by the Accounting Domain as inputs to answer questions created by accounting inquiries and reporting requirements. When considered comprehensively, these data will help both those inside and outside accounting see where the numbers come from and how they can be managed to improve cash performance.

The Foundation

SCT begins by modeling cash. Imagine putting a box around an entire company and modeling $cash_{IN}$, the rate of cash coming into the box, and $cash_{OUT}$, the rate of cash leaving (Exhibit 3.2). Focusing on $cash_{OUT}$ is of particular interest for SCT because it is the source of all costs, both cash and non-cash. $Cash_{OUT}$ comes from paying for something you've bought, such as capacity and services, or paying obligations such as taxes, fees, and royalties (TF&R).

For most companies, the largest cash expenditure is capacity. Capacity is what you buy in anticipation of demand or use. Typical types of capacity are space, labor, materials, and technology.[2] We consume this capacity for the purpose of doing work and creating output. While products and services provided to the market are types of output, they aren't the only types. Processed invoices, filed financial statements, R&D activities, planning budgets, and hired employees, too, are forms of output.

The entirety of these activities and their corresponding cash transactions comprise the OC Domain. All business activities and cash transactions occur here (Exhibit 3.3). Data regarding whether your company has truly made money, the amount of capacity it purchased, how it was

$ ——— $cash_{IN}$ ———→   Cash level   ———→ $cash_{OUT}$ ——— $

Exhibit 3.2 A box around the company (the $cash_{IN}$ $cash_{OUT}$ or CICO Border) helps define what does and doesn't affect cash. Whether you've made cash for a period is determined solely by considering what crossed the CICO border over a specified period. Also, if an improvement does not reduce $cash_{OUT}$, there are no cash savings. Note, cost accounting and the income statement has no such discipline regarding costs and cash

---

[2] See Yu-Lee, R.T. 2002. *Essentials of Capacity Management.* New York, NY: John Wiley and Sons.

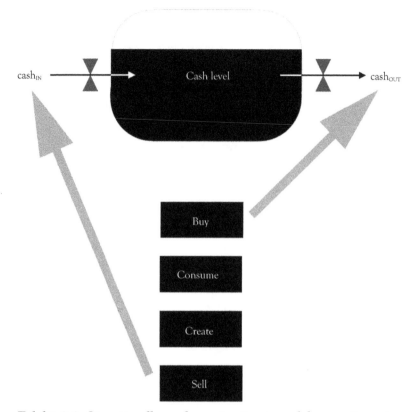

Exhibit 3.3 Operationally, we buy capacity, space, labor, equipment, materials, and as we pay for them, cash leaves the company. We then consume the capacity we bought to do work and create output. The output that is sold leads to revenue generation. This is the OC Domain

consumed, how efficiently and productively it was consumed, and what it created are all determined in the OC Domain.

When someone asks about the cost of a product or to perform a service or activity, this information is not natively available in the OC Domain. Answering that question requires the subjective and arbitrary data manipulation mentioned previously, that transform the OC Domain data into a different form than native OC Domain data. These transformed values create the information that comprises the Accounting Domain. Consider the following example.

Let's say you buy local phone service for $25, and with it, you get one month of access with no limits to the number or length of local calls you can make. If you want to make a long-distance call, however, it will cost 10¢ per minute. A 10-minute long distance call will cost $1. How much will a 10-minute local call cost?

There is an inherent challenge to answering the question. There is not enough information in what I gave you to create a reasonable and useful answer. The reason is, there is no relationship between what you bought, access, and how you use it, making calls. Ultimately, to calculate a cost, you will need to transform OC Domain data—$25 for access, 10-minute call—into a cost per minute or cost per call metric, which is Accounting Domain information. To do this, there will be subjective and arbitrary components used to create your answer.

Subjective

To calculate a cost, you will need to determine what data to include in the calculation; the scope. For instance, when calculating the cost of an activity, you will often need data and information such as labor rates or a proxy for labor rates and how long the activity took. For instance, if you pay someone $30 per hour and you want to determine her rate per minute, there are many ways to do so as was brought up in Chapter 1. You could divide the $30 by 60 minutes to create a 50¢ per minute cost rate. Similarly, to calculate a cost per call, you will need to calculate a rate per minute based on the access cost. However, what do you use for calls? Every minute of the month? If so, how many days do you consider for each month; 28, 29, 30, 31, 30.4 or 30.5?[3] Do you only consider the amount of time you're awake to make phone calls? How do you determine this with a reasonable degree of accuracy or precision? Do you only consider the times you most likely make phone calls? Only the time you spend on the phone? These are just a few of many possible questions that can, or should be addressed before calculating a cost per minute. It should be apparent that the process begins with a significant amount of subjectivity.

---

[3] 30.4 is the average number of days in a non-leap year. 30.5 is the average during a leap year.

Arbitrary

If you look at the cost of access in Exhibit 3.4, you will see that the cash cost, $25, and how it is used, making calls or consuming minutes, are mathematically independent. The cost that *should* depend on the length of calls does not change as the length of calls increases. Compare this to the curve for long distance where there is a relationship. The cost increases as the length increases.

To create a cost for a 10-minute call, you need a relationship between the access cost and how you use the access. Since no mathematical relationship exists, you will need to make up a relationship. Since the relationship is made up and connects two mathematically independent concepts, it is arbitrary. You can create a relationship between the number

With local calls, there is no relationship between the calls you make and what you pay. Hence, the two are mathematically independent.

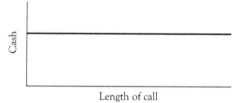

Cash paid, or to be paid, is directly influenced by the length of the long distance call. Hence. there is a dependent relationship between the cost and the length.

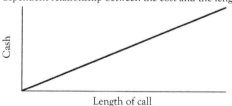

Exhibit 3.4 When you make a local call, no money leaves the CICO Border. This means there are no cash costs involved. Organizational capacity behaves this way. Consuming space, labor, material, or equipment you have purchased does not change the rate of cash leaving your company, unless there is a cash use charge involved with the purchase. If the costs you calculate for using capacity don't leave the CICO Border, they are not cash costs

of trees in your yard and the number of blue sedans in your neighborhood, but that doesn't mean the relationship has any validity. If you plant a new tree, that won't cause blue sedans to start showing up in your neighborhood just like buying a new sedan won't cause a tree to pop up in your backyard.

Hence, the cost of access and the number of calls made, or the length of calls made are no more mathematically related than the number of people at a baseball game in New York and the temperature in Saigon. Any math relationship you create between two mathematically independent subjects is mathematically arbitrary.

The Anatomy of the Transformation

To calculate a cost, we consider and capture data from the OC Domain (scope) and create a way to assign or allocate what is essentially capacity cost and use data, to the output it creates. The process is captured in Exhibit 3.5. The assignment/allocation process involves creating a relationship where there is none. Notice, we did not have to go through a transformation for the long-distance costs because a relationship existed.

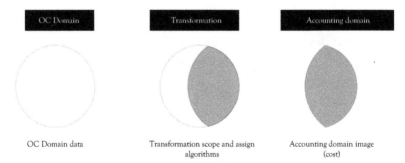

Exhibit 3.5 Creating Accounting Domain information is how cost accounting works. A subset of OC Domain data is taken and assigned or allocated to create an accounting image or cost. Notice, no new data come from this process. We are still using data available in the OC Domain. This process is a projection of what happens in the OC Domain into the Accounting Domain. By only having one dimension, the Accounting Domain, you're left with the task of projecting something that is 2-D into something that is 1-D. Doing so will often cause the loss of data and information

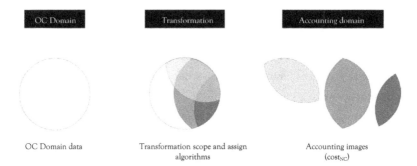

| OC Domain | Transformation | Accounting domain |

| OC Domain data | Transformation scope and assign algorithms | Accounting images (cost$_{NC}$) |

Exhibit 3.6 *By changing what OC Domain data you will use and how you will transform it, you will create different images or costs. This suggests calculated accounting costs are subject to the opinions of those who seek to determine it*

However, by changing the scope or the relationship (the assignment or allocation), you can create different images or costs as you can see in Exhibit 3.6.

This partially shows why calculated costs are not absolute. They can be manipulated and are subject to opinion. What scope should we use? How shall we assign costs? These are both questions where the answers rely on opinion. Hence, the costs they calculate, are based on, and therefore are, opinions.

This leads to another important fact about this transformation; the costs it calculates are no longer money. If calculated costs were money, we would see a cash transaction every time we make a local phone call in this instance. If we calculate the cost of a 10-minute local cost to be 5¢, for example, you do not spend 5¢ for each 10-minute call and you don't save 5¢ if you do not make the call. Recall, depending on the transformation approach, this cost could be 5¢, 4¢, 6.5¢ 1.3¢ or $5 (Exhibit 3.7). If the value were cash, this would not happen. As mentioned in Chapter 1, cash cannot change based on subjective criteria applied using arbitrary relationships. The $25 you paid for access was clear, distinct, and does not change based on opinion or what happens throughout the month.

This leads to a couple of important considerations. First, there are two types of costs, each introduced before; cash costs (cost$_C$) and non-cash costs (cost$_{NC}$). *All calculated accounting costs are cost$_{NC}$.* The output of all costing approaches, whether standard, activity-based, lean, or average, are all

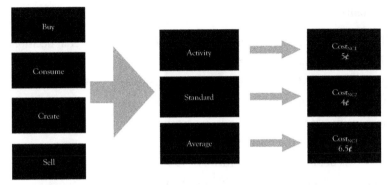

Exhibit 3.7 *Costing methodologies are all just transformation algorithms. Mathematically, they are basically the same. They all take OC Domain data and transform them into accounting images or costs. While one may claim to be more accurate than others, they all rely on arbitrary relationships to calculate this cost*

$cost_{NC}$. If you have to figure it out, it's likely not money. Second, calculated costs are not as bullet proof as we are led to believe. Part of the problem comes from the question being asked; "What does it cost?" and expectations we have from the response. There is no cost for a local call that is equivalent, money-wise, to the cost of a long-distance call although we expect them to be the same. The other part of the problem comes from the techniques used to answer the question, because the answer relies on the subjective notions and mathematically arbitrary relationships we discussed.

Implications

Buying capacity, in your company, is the same as buying local phone access. You buy space, you pay the rent, and it doesn't change with how you use it. You buy steel, you have it in inventory, and the cost, from a cash perspective, doesn't change with how you use it. You buy an X-ray machine, and the payments don't change with the X-rays you perform. The OC Domain is home to these data along with the cash transactions associated with running the business. However, historically, we've looked to the Accounting Domain to provide this information. Ultimately, the Accounting Domain fails to do so. This means we need a different way, different data and information to manage our companies if the goal is to make money.

Recommendation

The recommendation is to move from analyses and managerial decisions that reside primarily in the Accounting Domain to using the more comprehensive BDM framework. The BDM framework creates an effective alternative to analyses and management systems that focus solely on accounting information. This is an extremely important step that can ultimately enable full business transformation. Consider Toyota.

In his book, *Profit Beyond Measure*, Dr. Tom Johnson looks at the evolution of Toyota's Toyota Production System (TPS), sometimes known as just-in-time and the precursor to lean.[4] He compares it, and Toyota's success, to production philosophies and managerial approaches of US Big Three of GM, Ford, and Chrysler. He begins the book by talking about how Henry Ford was able to create a significant cost advantage by making only one version of the Model T at the famed River Rouge plant. When the need for variety ultimately ensued, there was a split in approaches on how to address the challenges.

There are challenges to creating variety on an assembly line such as Fords. Converting from making identical Model Ts to offering options or even different models would create significant disruption to an assembly line. Equipment changeovers to accommodate variety could take hours if not weeks. This, of course, would have implications on metrics such as efficiency and costs. To address the physical challenges and the desire to maintain product profitability targets, the Big 3 used accounting numbers to attempt to drive or influence the work. Since downtime from changeovers could be extensive, the idea was to produce each model or product in larger batches to take advantage of economies of scale. This would reduce unit costs, of course.

Each of the Big Three saw poor financial results. Toyota, on the other hand, was more profitable than all three combined. How? Johnson argues Toyota focused on the work, the means of production, while the Big Three focused on the results. By focusing on the means, Toyota minimized the

---

[4] Johnson, H.T., and A. Bröms. 2008. *Profit Beyond Measure: Extraordinary Results Through Attention to Work and People,* Chapter 1. London: Nicholas Brealey Publishing.

effects of model changeovers. For instance, if model changeovers took three minutes versus three days, many of the benefits of Henry Fords approach to mass production are maintained. Ultimately, by focusing on the efficient, effective, and productive use of capacity, Toyota achieved optimal financial results. However, by focusing on the results, the Big Three achieved suboptimal financial *and* operational results.

This experience aligns well with the suggestion here that we focus our managerial efforts on the OC Domain. The means Johnson discusses, where the work happens, is in the OC Domain. The results the Big Three sought and ultimately failed to achieve are in the Accounting Domain. When we open our analyses up to the entire organization we get a more comprehensive picture of business performance and how to improve it. By focusing on reducing changeover time, for instance, Toyota achieved the cost results they sought. By focusing on the cost targets, they sought, the Big Three arguably made enough of a mess that Toyota became the source of inspiration for people such as the CEO of Ford. Interestingly, when the CEO of Ford went to meet with Toyota to learn from them, the CEO of Toyota ironically thanked Henry Ford for teaching them what they needed to know.

Developing these thoughts, I'd like to propose the following steps related to transforming the operations and management of companies.

Use BDM to Model the Entire Company and as a Foundation for Managing the Means

The BDM model represents the entire organization (Exhibit 3.8) and all its operations, processes and cash transactions. This creates an unambiguous picture of all aspects of the organization including capacity levels, capacity consumption, efficiency, effectiveness, productivity, and output. It also creates insight into demand-type information such as what output was sold, how much was sold, and when money from sales is received.

Model and Highlight the Environment That Creates Costs

When modeling the organization's OC Domain, you capture all the data that are used to calculate costs. For instance, you have the $cost_C$ of capacity,

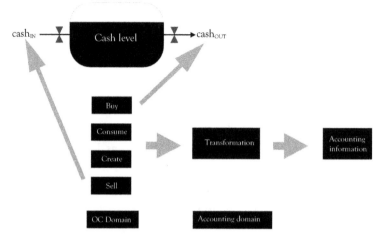

Exhibit 3.8 This is the Business Domain Management (BDM) framework. It is a model that represents the entire company and brings together both domains so that the relationship between the two can be understood and managed. The OC Domain represents all capacity and cash related activities. The Accounting Domain focuses on providing accounting information that should be used primarily for reporting

how much was purchased, and how it was used to create output. These are data that are native to the OC Domain. The cost transformation process uses a subset of these data with a particular allocation schema to calculate costs and create accounting information. Notice, no new data are created in the Accounting Domain. The Accounting Domain only uses OC Domain data, which are transformed into accounting information.

This helps explain why managing the means is better than managing the results. By improving performance in the OC Domain, you will see improvements in the Accounting Domain. If, by being more efficient, effective, and productive, you can get by with using and therefore buying 10,000 lbs of material versus 11,000, 25 people versus 30, or can lease 7,000 square feet of material versus 10,000, you will see improvements in your accounting information. Accounting Domain improvements most often result from changes made in the OC Domain, where better numbers create more desirable inputs into the calculation of Accounting Domain information. If that's the case, we really do not need Accounting Domain information for managerial purposes.

Table 3.1 If data are the raw numbers, information is the answer to queries using the raw data. All business data are captured on the OC Domain before a single cost is ever calculated. This suggests that from a data perspective, the Accounting Domain provides nothing new. There is, therefore, little, if any risk shifting out of the Accounting Domain to the OC Domain to capture data and manage the company

Data and information available outside the accounting domain	
Spend	Revenue
Did we make money/cash profit?	Output/production rate
Capacity levels/capacity purchased	Efficiency
Utilization	Demand
Productivity	Overproductive
Capacity to meet demand	Excess capacity consumed
Excess capacity purchased	Target spend
Potential increase in cash profit	Product service, customer capacity consumption

There may be apprehension when giving up accounting information for managerial purposes. There is usually concern from the perspective of losing information. How, for example, do you price without a product cost?[5] However, there are a significant amount of data and information available in the OC Domain before costs are calculated in the Accounting Domain. Table 3.1 offers a snapshot of some of the data and information that are available before calculating a single cost. This suggests that when shifting data and information requirements to the OC Domain from the Accounting Domain, there will be no loss of data. This results in the OC Domain being the more desirable domain to create accurate corporate and cash models.

---

[5] Leading practices in pricing suggest that prices should be a tied to the value of the product or service as perceived by the customer rather than to costs. See, for example, Baker, R.J. 2006. *Pricing on Purpose: Creating and Capturing Value*. New York, NY: John Wiley & Sons.

Data Not Affected by Accounting Conventions

One of the benefits of this approach is the notion that OC Domain data are not affected by accounting convention. The data exist prior to being subjected to the rules and conventions used for allocations, matching, accruals or any other ways to define, categorize, or account for activities and costs. Hence, by using these data, you have values that are in their native format, and unmanipulated by accounting techniques. Notice, one set of OC Domain data can create practically an infinite number of Accounting Domain representations. As such, it is often more effective to go to the source of the data for decision making rather than to one of many possible Accounting Domain images. I call using pre-processed data *getting ahead of accounting*.

Helps Describe and Resolve Conflicts Between Cash and Accounting Profit

One thing the BDM framework will highlight is the difference between cash and accounting profit. Cash profit reflects how much money was made in a period. It strictly considers cash inputs and outputs within the period. This is different from accounting profit, especially when it is accrual-based, which may use non-cash information, revenue recognition, and matching across periods; each of which may violate the rules of cash transactions.

Without a means to consider the impact to both cash and accounting profitability simultaneously, one may, for instance, improve accounting profit without realizing the negative cash implications of doing so. With proper insight, the implications of changes in both the OC Domain and the Accounting Domain can be considered and used as input to the final solution.

Enables Alignment Between Finance and Accounting

The BDM framework enables the creation of a comprehensive, organization-wide operations and cash model that supports the creation of accounting information. This model enables a common understanding, language, and set of measures and metrics that can be used by both accounting and operations. This creates enhanced opportunities to align the two groups and helps them manage the means so that they can create the desired financial results together. This, in turn, can lead to improvements in several areas including:

- Communication and cooperation between operations and accounting;
- Strategizing about what, how, and where to improve; and
- Understanding both the operational and financial impact of actions taken within the firm.

For example, instead of discussing negative variances, the two groups understand the operational source of the negative accounting variance (produced two fewer widgets last hour). The next step may be to consider whether the situation has relevance from a cash perspective (no extra money spent on labor or materials). They can talk about what, if any operational changes need to occur (no changes; output is within normal statistical variations), and whether the changes or lack of changes will have a negative effect on cash even if accounting profit will improve (no effect on cash or profit).

The next step is to delve into the theory behind Business Domain Management.

PART II

The Concept

CHAPTER 4

Introduction to Business Domain Management

The last three chapters have focused on the inability of accounting in general, and cost accounting specifically, to provide data and information that gives managers the best chance to reach the goal of making money. One way I describe the challenges faced by accounting is by imaging living in a two-dimensional world. Let's say this two-dimensional (2-D) world is a table top. As you stand on the tabletop, everything is either front-back (1-D) or left to right (1-D) for a total of two dimensions or 2-D. There is no up-down because that would require a third dimension, which doesn't exist to you.

Along comes a circle that shows up in your world (Exhibit 4.1). The circle was created by a sphere or a ball that intersected your table top. The resulting projection of the ball onto the table is a circle. What do you know about the ball? Practically nothing, because the ball is a three-dimensional object and you can only perceive 2-D space. All you have to go on is a circle that somehow appeared in your world.

Now, let's say your boss tells you to change the size of the circle. How would you do it? Without knowing how it got there, you can do little to change it. What created the circle in the first place has already occurred, and why it occurred is beyond your ability to comprehend. You might come up with ways to make it appear to be different, but you cannot change what physically happened with the ball. To understand the circle and how to change it, you need the third dimension, the up-down dimension, so you can now comprehend the ball and, therefore, the situation that created the circle.

Once you have the up-down dimension, you will understand the situation. You see the ball, how it intersects your world, and how the image, the circle, had been created. Now you realize the only way to change

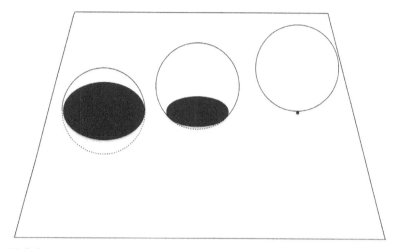

Exhibit 4.1 As the ball intersects the plane, an image is created. The only way to change the image projected onto the plane is to change what created it. Likewise, accounting costs are projections from operations and cash activities and data. To improve the accounting numbers, you must change what created them

the circle is to move the ball, assuming your world is stationary. If you could move the ball up or down in the third dimension, it will affect the size of the circle image in the 2-D world. Said differently, sometimes the changes that need to be made to get the results in a particular space or world must come from outside that space. In the case of BDM, reduced costs in the Accounting Domain will come from changes made in the OC Domain.

The business environment is similar to this scenario when we live in the world of accounting information. When you see a cost, say $13.29, what can you tell from it? Do you know what capacity was involved? Do you know how it was consumed? The answer, by and large, is "no." The reason? The situation, and the data responsible for creating the cost, happened outside of accounting. Transforming OC Domain data into the Accounting Domain will create a loss of data similar to the information about the ball that is lost when the circle is projected onto the table. The cost is like the circle. It is a projection, or an image created when OC Domain data are projected into the Accounting Domain.

Key information necessary to understand the cost is lost in the cost transformation process because of the steps involved when calculating the cost. For example, suppose I told you a unit cost calculated one way was $2.50 and calculated another way was $3. If you wanted to reduce this cost, where would you focus and how much would your suggestion reduce this cost?

Without knowing where the cost came from, you're limited in your ability to figure out what to do. You'd likely start with efficiency but what effect would it have? Now, if I told you for the $2.50 cost, you have a person who makes $30 per hour and she makes a unit of output every five minutes, you can see your options to improve the calculated cost. You could either pay her or someone else less or shorten her processing time. In the case of the $3 cost, the same $30 per hour person makes about 10 units per hour. Now, you can focus on the capacity cost, the processing time, or the reason she produces 10 in an hour when she could theoretically make 12. Once we have data from another dimension as context, the situation becomes easier to comprehend. This is another reason managing the means makes more sense than managing the results. By focusing on the means, you have more levers to pull. Trying to manage results leaves you in a position of trying to guess how and where to make changes. The tail is wagging the dog, so to speak.

Strategic cost transformation is about using BDM to create the equivalent of a multidimensional approach for operations, cash, cost, and profit management. Accounting needs another dimension for cost management to be effective corporate-wide. The basic idea begins by breaking up a company into two business domains; the Accounting Domain and the Operations and Cash (OC) Domain.

The Accounting Domain represents all accounting information. When someone asks about costs and profit in a more general sense, they are focused on the Accounting Domain. Hence, any data related to the cost of output exists in the Accounting Domain as do all of the financial statements. This is the table. The second domain is the Operations and Cash Domain or OC Domain. All business activity occurs in the OC Domain. The OC Domain is the ball. This is where capacity is bought and consumed, output is created, salable output is sold, and cash is collected. Since buying and selling occurs in the OC Domain and since these are the primary drivers of $cash_{IN}$ and $cash_{OUT}$ transactions, the subsequent modeling of cash also occurs in the OC Domain.

By combining the OC Domain with the Accounting Domain, you now have a complete picture of your business. You know your spending and infrastructure cash cost data, the size, capability, consumption and output from your business infrastructure, and when and why cash was spent. These data, then, can be fed into the transformation algorithms responsible for generating the information used in the Accounting Domain.

Business domains are separate and distinct, and it's important to understand which domain you're referring to in conversations within your firm. Not doing so can create confusion and lead to bad decision making. There are a number of scenarios where one can increase cash at the expense of accounting profit and vice versa, so it's important to be aware of what is going on and why, so you can minimize the impact. Calculated costs and profit are Accounting Domain concepts that do not represent cash. However, by assuming they are cash, it's possible to make decisions to improve profit that lead to a loss of cash.

When you mix OC and Accounting Domains you're operating in mixed domain mode, where one may confuse, or not separate the domains. For instance, I was speaking to a leader of a professional services firm, and I asked her about a few managerial objectives they had in place. She explained how they looked to assign costs more accurately and then update pricing to improve margins and to make more money.

This is a classic example of being in mixed domain mode. If you are in a service environment where an employee's time can be assigned to multiple customers or in a manufacturing environment where capacity can be split among multiple products and you'd like to assign cost to a customer or a product, you sit quite squarely in the Accounting Domain. The idea of calculating a margin, too, was in the Accounting Domain, as her firm used cost-plus pricing. She assumed the concepts of profit and making money could be mixed together legitimately like jambalaya. However, unbeknownst to her, they were confusing her understanding of what was really going on in her company and as a result, limiting her options to act.

Concepts such as costs, profits, cash assignments, and efficiency should be kept in their respective domains. If she wants to make money, she should focus on the OC Domain where cash transactions and the business activities that affect cash occur. In other words, focus on the ball, not the circle. This is where the means are, where capacity is bought, output is sold, and $cash_{IN}$ and $cash_{OUT}$ are subsequently affected. Cost assignments affect neither $cash_{IN}$ or $cash_{OUT}$ directly. By focusing on cost assignments, she was only affecting the image projected into the Accounting Domain, the circle, which affects $cash_{OUT}$ only if the new assignments affect taxable margins which, then, affect taxes paid.

Pricing is another example of confusing modes. Price *should* be an OC Domain issue. Price should reflect the value of your offering to the market. You can't sell a new $45,000 Yugo. The cost to manufacture or offer a service is not a part of this value equation. How often does the cost to the company of what you buy enter the pricing conversation or your buying calculus? Rarely. If you have a leak at home and it requires an emergency repair, what the plumber is paid probably doesn't matter to you. The fact she can save you from significant damage and inconvenience does. The price is tied to what you are willing or able to pay to offset the damage and inconvenience.

As you learn about domains, guidance regarding what concepts reside in which might be useful. To help provide insight into what concepts belong in which domain, please refer to Table 4.1.

There are areas where it is less clear what domain you're operating in. I often hear executives discussing cost reduction for instance. Without an understanding of the difference between $cost_C$ and $cost_{NC}$, they may assume they're the same; cost reduction is cost reduction. When this happens, the objective is to gain clarity regarding whether they're talking about saving money or improving margins. Money, which is $cost_C$, affects $cash_{OUT}$ and therefore resides in the OC Domain. Improving margins, which is $cost_{NC}$, does not affect $cash_{OUT}$, and resides in the Accounting Domain. The former involves changing isocash curves and the latter involves moving down the same isocash curve as described in Exhibits A–D in Chapter 3.

The next step is to take you more deeply into the OC domain, along with an emphasis on understanding and managing capacity and cash.

Table 4.1 Much of what we're grown used to actually exists in the OC Domain meaning it has not been subject to Accounting Domain transformations. When having conversations and performing analyses, it's important to discern which domain you're in and confine the discussion or analysis to that domain

OC Domain	Accounting domain
$Cost_{IN}, Cost_{OUT}$	Product, service, activity costs
Cash costs	Margins (product, service, customer, company)
Cash profit	Inventory value
Capacity	Recognized revenue
Capacity consumption	Fixed and variable costs
Efficiency, productivity, effectiveness	Variances
Value pricing	Cost plus pricing

CHAPTER 5

Understanding the OC Domain

The first BDM domain I'll focus on is the OC Domain. The OC Domain, the means, is where all business and cash transactions and activities occur, and it is also where I think most business analyses should occur. This is where Toyota focused. This suggestion may be putting the cart ahead of the horse a bit as it relates to the context of this book, but by addressing it now, I hope to help you create a connection between what happens in the OC Domain and what typical analyses often focus on. This should create context for why we should focus more on the OC Domain and the means, when we delve more deeply into business analyses.

The OC Domain is composed of two parts; the Cash Dynamics Framework and the Business Operations Framework. The Cash Dynamics Framework describes how cash flows into and out of a company, and how cash levels change. The Business Operations Framework models a company's infrastructure and business operations, activities, and processes, and provides context for the Cash Dynamics Framework. Together, they create a holistic perspective of operations and cash performance. Let's discuss both.

The Cash Dynamics Framework specifically focuses on modeling a company's cash transactions. If you put a box around your company as described in Chapter 3 and measure the cash coming in and the cash going out during a period, you will be able to model the company's cash dynamics. At any time, if you have a beginning cash amount, and you consider both $cash_{IN}$ and $cash_{OUT}$ over an arbitrarily selected period, you will know how much money you will have at the end of the period and how it has changed over the analysis period.

$Cash_{IN}$ is money the company receives and can be placed into its coffers. This money comes primarily from sales, but there can be other sources such as money received from loans. Cash$_{OUT}$ occurs when money is being paid and, therefore, leaves the company. This usually happens for one of three reasons; purchased capacity, services, and obligations such as taxes, fees, and royalties (TF&R).

When you pick an analysis period, the sole determinants of whether cash increases or decreases is the difference between cash$_{IN}$ and cash$_{OUT}$ during the period. When the difference is positive, the level of cash increases. When negative, it decreases. There are no other data that are more material, accurate, or precise measures of whether you are making or losing money than this difference. This model also sets the stage for modeling organizational improvements. When looking to improve cash performance, you must change cash$_{IN}$, cash$_{OUT}$, or the relative difference between the two. This will be discussed in some detail in Chapter 17.

The Business Operations Framework describes how business occurs. There are four components of the Business Operations Framework; what we buy, how we consume it, what we create, and what we sell (Exhibit 5.1). Each of these is discussed in more detail in Chapter 7.

Together, these four areas create the foundation for the Business Operations Framework. Any company and any business activity can be

Exhibit 5.1 The basic activities of the OC Domain are buying (mostly capacity), using capacity to create output, and when it's an option, selling the output to generate revenue

modeled in the context of this framework, and a significant amount of information can be gleaned from it. You know how much capacity you bought and have, and how much of it was used. From this, you can get efficiency information. You know what was created and how effectively capacity was used to do so, which allows you to understand output and determine whether the capacity was used appropriately. You know how much work your infrastructure is able to create and where to focus to improve. In other words, this provides the basis for managing the means.

When combined, the cash dynamics and Business Operations Frameworks create the OC Domain, which is the basis for all business activities and financial transactions. Center to all this is capacity and capacity management. Being the focal point of spending and work, managing it is the key to any company looking to manage costs and make money.

CHAPTER 6

The Case for Capacity Management

Ultimately, we are all focused on The Goal; making money. The key question is, are we focusing on the right things to ensure we're making money? I'd like to argue that, by and large, we are not. To manage money, we should model it, so we can see what is coming into and leaving the company, and how that affects how much money we have at any given moment. One of the most influential reasons money leaves an organization is paying for capacity it has purchased. Recall, capacity is what you buy in anticipation of demand or use. This includes space, labor, materials, equipment, and technology.

Capacity, then, should be the at the center of practically all financial and operational analyses. Whether you're making money or you're profitable will be influenced by how much capacity you have, how it's used, and what was created and sold. When making improvements to processes via techniques such as lean and six-sigma, buying new IT solutions, or hiring consultants, you will find that the nature of the operational improvement will center on capacity, and the financial changes they enable are affected by capacity. Hence, managing capacity should be the center of our analyses, but it isn't. Hourly labor capacity, for instance is often considered and modeled as direct labor in accounting analyses. Proof is found in the desire to focus on how it affects costs and profit as a variable cost even though its output is independent of what you paid to have it. We rarely look at space costs the same way we look at material, equipment, or labor costs even though, mathematically, and notionally from both operational and financial perspectives, they all behave the same as it relates to cash.

I would posit capacity is the most important and least understood aspect of business. As such, leaders make bad decisions with factors that are capacity related. Consider Toyota as a positive example. Arguably, the means Dr. Johnson referred to was primarily capacity management. By reducing changeover times, for instance, Toyota could manage machine capacity uptime as all as others managed around it by producing in large batches. This ultimately allowed Toyota to produce in much greater variety, in smaller batches, and in a much more cost-efficient manner than their competitors. Companies that were focused on results put their efforts into other areas that led to poor capacity management. For instance, instead of reducing setup time, they focused on buying faster equipment to reduce costs and maintain efficiency. If a machine is down due to changeovers, buy faster machines to make up for the downtime rather than eliminating that which causes downtime—lengthy changeovers. As Einstein said, a clever person solves a problem. A wise person avoids it.

Ultimately, our decision making is severely impaired with improperly modeled cost reduction analyses, make versus buy analyses, which lead to bogus value propositions, and investments in improvement opportunities and solutions such as IT projects that don't realize the promised benefit.

To truly understand capacity, there are four ideas to understand about capacity:

1. The definition
2. It's importance
3. The operating dynamics
4. The cash dynamics

The first two will be covered in this chapter. The operating dynamics of capacity will be covered in Chapter 7, while the cash dynamics will be the focus of Chapter 8.

Defining Capacity

In my book, *Essentials of Capacity Management* I defined capacity as what a company buys in anticipation of use or demand. If we think of capacity this way, it is what companies spend most of their money on. As mentioned earlier in the chapter, capacity includes space, labor, materials, equipment, and technology. Said differently, this is your office, factory, and warehouse locations that you are paying to lease or buy. It is all of the people who work for your firm. It does not only include the materials that go into products you make and sell, but the materials we consume in office work each day, and the inventory we have for operating equipment to minimize downtimes in case of a failure or repair. It includes the tools we used to perform work, such as MRI machines in healthcare, cranes and bulldozers in construction, planes in transportation, and stamping machines in fabrication. Finally, technology such as computers and servers, networks, and software, too, are types of capacity.

One way to think about capacity is to reconsider the local phone service example. We bought a month for $25 thinking we may or will need to use it sometime throughout the month. All capacity has the same attributes. We buy a certain amount, we consume some or all of what we bought, and this consumption leads to work output. Another key attribute is that what we buy and pay cash for doesn't change with how we use it. We can calculate a cost per local call, for instance, but the $25 in cash we pay for local service remains the same whether we make calls or not. Similarly, neither the cash cost for salaries or rent change when consumed.

One important concept to understand as we define capacity is, it exists solely in the OC Domain. What you buy, how much you spend, what you do with it, and what it creates are native OC Domain attributes and data. The cash used to buy capacity affects the rate of cash$_{OUT}$. What it creates that is sold forms the basis for the rate of cash$_{IN}$. Hence, to understand capacity and to manage it effectively, the only way you can do so is to have an OC Domain model of capacity.

Understanding the Importance of Capacity

As mentioned previously, capacity is critically important to your business, and there are three reasons why I believe this is the case. First, capacity is likely your largest expenditure. When considering the entirety of what comprises capacity, that's where your money is most likely going. Second, capacity is the basis for how most work is completed; the means. We buy capacity, we consume it, and create output. Whether making widgets in a factory using people, equipment, and materials we've purchased or performing surgery using people, space, and equipment, the capacity we buy is center to the completion of practically all work. This is where Toyota focused, which led to a significant competitive advantage. Finally, it creates the foundation for all financial data in both the OC Domain and the Accounting Domain. Being the largest expenditure, it has a greater effect on cash$_{OUT}$ than anything else in the business. This means any analyses that occur in the OC Domain and are focused on cash must consider capacity. In the Accounting Domain, costs are often calculated considering the cost of capacity and how it was consumed. For instance, calculating a cost per customer service call, you'd consider the wages of the employee (capacity) and the number of calls or length of the call (output). Most situations where an allocation or assignment must be used involves creating a cost for the output of capacity.

Since capacity is a very important aspect of a business, it is essential to understand what it is and how it works. This enables you to make decisions in the OC Domain to get the financial results you want in both domains; manage the means to achieve the results. The next two chapters will go into the operational dynamics of capacity and the financial dynamics of capacity. This will help create an understanding of how to manage capacity to achieve desired targets while avoiding accounting-centric pitfalls that happen when capacity dynamics are ignored.

CHAPTER 7

Fundamentals of Capacity Dynamics

As mentioned in Chapter 6, capacity is one of the largest, most pervasive, and arguably most ignored aspects of an organization. The purpose of this chapter is to increase the awareness of the operational dynamics of capacity so that it can be managed more effectively. By operational dynamics, I mean how capacity functions within your organization. This is critical when thinking about, planning, and managing capacity; the means. How you use capacity and the demand for it can affect how much you need and, therefore, how much you buy. This, of course, affects $cash_{OUT}$ when pay for what you buy.

Ideally, you will want appropriate supporting capacity metrics that describe how to use capacity and create output. These metrics should help you strike a balance between being efficient, effective, and productive. Being efficient allows you to create more output at a given level of input or the same output with less input. Making ten widgets in one hour is more efficient than making nine. However, efficiency isn't enough, as the Big 3 found. Efficiency in the absence of being effective and productive can lead to poor managerial decisions and corporate results. Being effective and productive means you are using your capacity to do what is needed by your firm and the market, and no more. As defined in this book, effectivity and productivity have a component of aligning output with demand that efficiency does not have. Hence, focusing on efficiency alone can cause companies to buy or produce more than demand dictates, leading to poorer cash performance.

Every capacity type has the same operational attributes:

1. You buy it
2. You consume it
3. You create output

Let's consider each in the context of improving organizational performance.

Buying Capacity

When you buy capacity, you buy a fixed amount of it for a price. For instance, when leasing space, you may pay $20,000 for 5,000 ft² for a month. With labor, you buy an hour, day, week, month, or year for a fixed price. With materials, you buy so many pieces, kilograms, liters, or meters of materials. Since the amount of capacity you buy is fixed, I sometimes refer to it as static capacity. I also synonymously use the term input capacity because they are inputs for creating work.

If you believe your costs are high and you want to know where money is going, look at the levels of input capacity you're buying. There is a direct relationship between the input capacity you buy and cash$_{OUT}$, which is a function of when and how you pay for the input. When you are inefficient, ineffective, or unproductive with your capacity, you may need to buy more to meet demand. This information is not found, nor is it comprehensively available on the income statement. You may find some evidence in cash flow statements and the balance sheet, but the story is not as clear as if you just looked at the rate of cash leaving your firm because demand, the key element, is not a consideration in accounting reports.

Overproduction can lead to the need for excess capacity, as artificially high demand and subsequent output levels may require higher levels of capacity to process. The efficient use of capacity allows for more to get done with less input, hence, by using it wisely, you can get away with meeting demand with lower levels of capacity and, therefore, lower cash costs. The problem is, accounting can hide this excess labor or material capacity. It may show up, for instance, as a negative variance or may end up on the balance sheet as excess inventory. Excessive equipment purchases are hidden in depreciation values. This keeps you from seeing the immediate and periodic cash impact of decisions you make.

Overbuying capacity in the name of purchasing economies of scale, too, is an issue. Faced with lower unit price options, there is a tendency to focus on the deal rather than on the money being spent. Three for five dollars seems like a better deal than one for two dollars even when there is only demand for one or two. Emphases should be placed on both the demand for what you're buying, and the cash spent.

There is a tendency with capacity to shift understanding, interpretation, and metrics to the Accounting Domain. For instance, if we lease 5,000 ft^2 of space for $20,000, you may be tempted to describe it as $4 per square foot. However, it is not $4 per square foot in the OC Domain. This is an Accounting Domain metric. In the OC Domain, you simply paid $20,000 for 5,000 ft^2. It is not broken down into smaller units, square feet in this case, because you were not buying by the square foot, you are buying a combined 5,000 ft^2. The $4 per square foot is a transformation of OC Domain data to create an Accounting Domain metric.

Consume Units of Capacity

Once we have the static capacity, the idea is to consume it with tasks or work. The factory worker builds widgets just like the construction worker executes building and improvement projects. Medical staff treat patients. This may be how we typically think of capacity, but it is limiting. The laborer is no different from a customer service rep, an HR manager, a finance director, or the CEO. You buy access and you consume them to perform work. Similarly, they are no different from the space you rent and consume, the computer processing and storage space you buy and consume, or the 10,000 pounds of steel you buy and convert to finished products.

As mentioned before, with input capacity, you pay for access to a certain number of capacity units and you consume what you bought. If you buy 10,000, pounds you consume pounds as you create output. If you buy eight hours, you consume hours as you perform work. If you buy 5,000 ft^2 of space, you consume square feet creating offices, performing operations and work, or storing items.

As you perform work, there is one truth. Think about the ball and the table. That intersection yields one answer no matter how you may want to represent it. Similarly, how much capacity the work consumed is, in retrospect, unambiguous. For instance, if you spent 30 minutes on a conference call, *that* you spent 30 minutes is unambiguous. Reporting what you did may include inaccuracies. For instance, if you're required to keep track of, and document your time for reporting purposes, you may not report the 30 minutes accurately. However, the fact remains, you physically spent 30 minutes on the call whether you reported it accurately or not. This is important when understanding the use of capacity.

Output Capacity

When you buy 10,000 pounds of steel, that is input capacity; what you start with. Output capacity is what you can and do create with the input. For instance, if each product manufactured requires two pounds of steel, you can create 5,000 units, theoretically, from the steel you bought. That is the production output capacity of the steel in the context of making that particular product. Another product or combination of products can, and often will, create different levels of output capacity from the same amount of input. Because output levels can change, it is also referred to as dynamic capacity.

Output capacity, and the difference between output and input capacity, is very important to understand and manage because their interplay will decide how well your company performs both operationally and financially. Input capacity is what you buy and spend money on. Output capacity is what you can create from the input you bought. For instance, you hire a laborer for one day for $240. What you bought for the $240 is eight hours. That is input. Now you have her begin answering phones at a rate of five per hour. What you get from her, five calls per hour, is output. If the five phone calls consume an entire hour and that is the most she could possibly handle, that is her maximum output capacity. However, if she can handle more calls, the five is her realized output capacity and her maximum is a higher number.

When you focus on improvements such as buying new computers, software, equipment, you implement lean, or execute Six Sigma projects, the focus is typically on improving output and output capacity. In the same hour, call screening software may increase her output to eight calls from five. This is more output (8) at the same input level (one hour). There is a tendency to capture improvements like these as cost savings. However, input capacity, what you spent money on, has not changed. Hence, there are $cost_{NC}$ savings, but not $cost_C$ savings because you're still on the same isocash curve and $cash_{OUT}$ was not affected. The input capacity cost creates the cash basis for the isocash curve and output just moves you along the curve. Improving the output of input capacity just means you have increased efficiency, not saved money.

Mathematically, efficiency is just the ratio of output to input. For instance, you buy one gallon of gas. That is input. You drive 20 miles, output, and consume the gallon of gas. Your fuel efficiency is 20 miles for one gallon of gas or 20 miles per gallon. A more efficient car may travel 30 miles for each gallon. Fuel efficiency takes the output, distance traveled, and divides it by the input, one gallon. The same concept works with all other types of capacity. If our employees can increase the number of calls they can handle in a period of time, what we bought, time, has not changed, but the output has, and efficiency has improved as a result.

Let's assume a gallon of gas costs $4. You can calculate a cost per mile of 20¢ when getting 20 miles per gallon. The cost per mile decreases to 13.3¢ as efficiency increases to 30 miles per gallon, but what you paid, $4 cash, did not change. Same numbers, different information. The cost per mile is $cost_{NC}$, and it decreases as efficiency increases. This isn't a coincidence. The cost per mile is just the math inverse of efficiency.

$$\epsilon = \text{output} \div \text{input (ex. 20 miles} \div \$4 \text{ investment in gas)} \qquad (7.1)$$

$$\epsilon^{-1} = \text{input} \div \text{output (e.g., } \$4 \text{ investment} \div 20 \text{ miles)}$$

Hence, increasing efficiency is the source of a lower cost per unit.

Consider the phone answering example. The input capacity we bought from a labor perspective was time. It is the denominator in the efficiency equation. The calls made comprise the numerator. For maximum output capacity, assume in one hour, she is able to make eight versus her usual five calls. You can see improvements in both efficiency and cost per hour by increasing output. If she makes $30 per hour, and through improvement her efficiency has increased to eight calls for $30 from five calls for the same $30. The cost per call will decrease to $3.75 from $5, again, with no change to cash.

The key, though, is whether there is demand for eight. If the improvement is made and there is no demand for eight calls, the improvement does not do a lot for you directly. Although she can make eight with her time, only five may be needed. The manifestation is that capacity is being made available that would have otherwise been consumed (Exhibit 7.1). This excess capacity can be used by other activities, eliminated, or left alone.

This suggests improvements such as lean and ERP solutions will not often improve cash directly with their proposed improvements. They target output and what you bought was input. To have a financial effect, you will have to shift to a lower isocash curve by changing what you buy. This is what focusing on the means bought for Toyota. They had a lower cost to meet demand, suggesting they operated on a lower cost curve relative to their competitors. The objective is to make decisions that affect cash$_{OUT}$. The changes necessary to reduce cash costs will not happen on

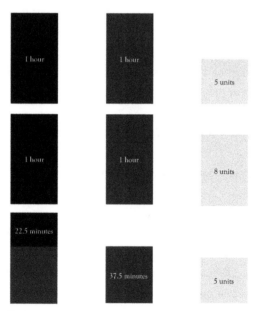

Exhibit 7.1 By increasing efficiency, output levels can be met while consuming less capacity. This will free capacity to be available for other purposes

their own. They require purposeful acts, enabled by improvements, that will cause the change (covered in Chapter 17). Understanding the cash dynamics will explain why.

A Few Words on Time Sheets

My friend Ron Baker asked if my position on capacity suggests I'm an advocate for time sheets. One could conclude that given my interests in capacity consumption rates. However, I'm against their use. Here's why.

I liken capacity utilization and management to looking at your property and its landscaping. If you stand across the street and look at your house, you can see whether there is a balance or not with the trees, shrubs, or decorative pieces you're looking at. From here, you can plan your next steps; what else do you need to buy, where are you going to put it, or how are you going to use it. You may also observe something that is out of place or something you may need to look at in more detail as it relates to all other factors. You're looking at the big picture and how things relate to one another, and then comparing them to what you consider desirable.

The question is, if you're looking to manage the big picture in this scenario, would standing in the yard counting trees, shrubs, or blades of grass provide you with a better understanding of what you're trying to manage? Would you understand how beautifully or effectively you'd designed your landscape? No. There seems to be a point below which detailed data fail to provide a better understanding of the whole system. As Stuart Kauffman, an author and leading thinker in the area of complexity noted, when studying living systems, which some argue businesses are, "[l]ife…[emerges] whole and has always remained whole. Life, in this view is not to be located in its parts, but in the collective emergent properties of the whole they create."[1] He also states, "In all these cases, the order that emerges (from the living system), depends on robust and typical properties of the systems, than on the details of structure and function."

When we start looking at parts of an 8-hour shift, we lose track of what we are supposed to be managing. It's easy to get caught up expending

---

[1] Kauffman, S. 1996. *At Home in the Universe: The Search for the Laws of Self-Organization and Complexity*, 24. Cambridge, MA: Oxford University Press.

resources to adjust individual blades of grass that seem out of place when viewed closely. However, in the bigger picture, they don't distract from what you're trying to accomplish and are hardly noticeable. What does knowing how much time someone spent in the bathroom or talking to a friend tell you about how productive they were overall? What's important is the whole; given the level of capacity that exists, how much output was it able to create? Was it enough, too much, or not enough compared to demand? Was it considered valuable to the market? Those are the most important first questions. With the right tools and perspective, you can easily see whether you have problems with capacity levels, consumption, processes, or procedures, all from this simple question and subsequent analysis.

Managing by time sheets is akin to Johnson's managing by results. The objective should be to consider the previous questions, identify high level issues, understand how work is done and to eliminate waste found when performing the work; manage and improve the means. If you do that, output improvement opportunities should be created. Keeping detailed track of time doesn't fix anything. It doesn't improve the process; it just reports "what was," but only in a perfect world. The world of time sheets is far from perfect, however. Consider these factors why I believe time sheets should not be the focus to managerial activity.

1. The information is rarely truthful. When you fill out time sheets, how often do you guess or fudge numbers? Now, what if everyone guessed or fudged (my guess is that most do), how truthful and reliable will the information you have be? Did they *really* spend that much time doing productive work on those particular tasks?

2. They are not needed for costs. First, the costs calculated with this information are $cost_{NC}$, so they are not money, and are a function of how the cost is calculated. This means knowing this number doesn't provide insight into how much money you've made when price is factored in. Second, while you're working on the third decimal of precision to bill a client, "does it cost $2.346 or $2.347," a different set of assumptions or costing schema can calculate a cost of $2.90. Third, how accurate is the cost if the numbers used to calculate the cost were fudged?

3. There are questionable returns. How much time, effort, and money are spent trying to process time sheet data, review it, and then manage based on the output? In many cases, there are systems involved, people who process and review the data, create and review reports, and then there is the time everyone spends trying to figure out, recall, or fudge the time they put into the system every week or two. Again, the data are often fudged and we're looking at non-cash information being created. Having this information doesn't tell you whether you have an effective system, and in many cases, the specific conditions that caused time problems to occur may be gone as well, so it isn't as though you can go back and fix what was apparently broken. Hence, one should ask themselves how prudent it is to invest so heavily in information that has questionable value.

The ultimate objective, as stated earlier, is to create output consuming the least amount of capacity. By stepping back and looking at the bigger picture of your system versus looking under a microscope, you will be able to see what is good and where improvement opportunities exist within your system. Again, this can happen without time sheets. If a report that should take hours takes days, there is a sign that something is wrong. Walking up to someone and asking her what caused the delay will likely, in a trustworthy working environment, create the information necessary to know the situation and address the situation. Answers such as, the computer was down, didn't have the right information, the report was 9th on the priority list, or she forgot to do it may result, but you now know what happened. With the right approach, these are answers that can be identified, and addressed without a single time sheet being created or processed.

CHAPTER 8

The Cash Dynamics of Capacity

In Chapter 7, we talked about the differences between input, or static capacity, and output or dynamic capacity. One of the key differences is that you buy input, not output capacity. When you hire a manager, you are buying her time, not her decisions. This gives you access to her decisions, but you are not paying her on a decision-by-decision basis. Of course, when you buy input capacity, you must pay for it, creating the tie between input capacity and cash. Given the notion that most companies are fundamentally capacity based, it should follow that most of what the company pays for is capacity. If that is true, *then the largest influence of cash, specifically cash$_{OUT}$ is capacity.* That makes understanding the relationship between capacity and cash dynamics and what levers you have to manage them critical. To reach the goal and to make money for the firm, you will have to get your arms around the cash dynamics of capacity. When you understand the dynamics, you will make decisions knowing, in foresight and more precisely, what the impact will be on cash. You will not be bamboozled by huge value propositions that have no basis in cash.

To create this understanding, I'd like to take you through the three key points to understand about the cash dynamics of capacity.

Point 1: Buying Input

As mentioned last chapter, when we buy input capacity, there is an exchange of cash for capacity. For instance, we exchange $60,000 salary for one year of work. This purchase and the terms set the stage for cash$_{OUT}$.

One challenge to managing input is keeping it and the cash dynamics in the OC Domain. Capacity and the related cash dynamics belong in the OC Domain where they are created and are unperturbed by the subjectivity and arbitrary actions that are a part of the transformation into the Accounting

Domain. Once the data are transformed into the Accounting Domain, you will lose insight into the cash and operational dynamics of capacity. As mentioned previously, when you consider a product cost, you have no idea, when looking at the cost, how much capacity you bought as a firm, or what you paid for it, which are critical to know from a cash perspective.

Point 2: Are Capacity Costs Fixed or Variable?

One key attribute, perhaps the most important one, is the notion that *capacity costs do not change with use.* Consider leased space. The $20,000 you pay for 5,000 ft² of space does not change with how you use it or how much of it you consume. The same holds true for all other types of capacity. For instance, consider labor where a person is paid by the hour. If you agree to pay her $30 for an hour of work, that amount does not change with what she does in that hour. Whether the job entails making widgets, cleaning floors, processing invoices, hiring new employees or making executive decisions, what you pay her does not change with her level of consumption or output.

Let's recap. I mentioned a laborer's cash costs do not change with output. They are fixed with respect to output. I expanded this to all forms of capacity. If you agree with me on this, then we have a problem. In the Accounting Domain, direct materials and direct labor are considered variable costs. A variable cost, by definition in the accounting world, is a cost that varies with output. Long distance calls are variable cash costs. The cost of the call changes directly with minutes, and the more we speak, the more it costs. However, capacity is like the local call, not long distance. It doesn't matter how many calls we make or how long they are, the $cost_C$ cost is still $25.

This creates a major disagreement between cash and the OC Domain data and cost information in the Accounting Domain. Accounting says these costs vary and cash say they do not. This is an issue that companies, which deal with fixed and variable costs, must understand. The costs that vary are $cost_{NC}$, so while the cost may change in the Accounting Domain, the cash cost in the OC Domain is unaffected.

Capacity costs do vary, however, just not with output, which is the next point.

Point 3: Capacity Costs Only Change with Price or the Amount of Input Capacity Purchased

One thing I regularly hear from cost accounting advocates is that all costs vary. Well, yes, they do. Both $cost_C$ and $cost_{NC}$ vary. The question is, what do they vary with respect to? In the Accounting Domain, direct labor and material costs vary with output. In the OC Domain, they don't. Why is that?

With capacity, you are not buying output, you're buying input. As such, the amount you pay, $cost_C$ is a function of how much input you buy and what you pay for it. For instance, if you buy eight hours of labor at $30 per hour, you spend $240. This is more, of course, than if you buy eight hours of labor at $25 per hour. Likewise, buying six hours at $30 is cheaper than buying eight hours at $25 per hour. Hence, capacity costs do vary, but not for the reasons accounting variable costs vary. When you buy more capacity the $cash_{OUT}$ increases, which is an increased cash cost to your firm. When you buy less or cheaper capacity, $cash_{OUT}$ decreases.

There are several key business implications of this when considering the cash dynamics of capacity.

1. All cash and capacity data are native to the OC Domain.
2. Increasing efficiency will not directly improve cash costs.
3. Isocash curve shifts are tied to how much capacity you are buying or the price you pay (Exhibits A-D in Chapter 3).
4. The only way to reduce $cost_C$ from a capacity perspective is to buy less of it, buy cheaper, or both.

Native Data

As mentioned earlier, all capacity and cash data as they relate to $cash_{IN}$ and $cash_{OUT}$, and the respective analyses belong in the OC Domain. Of course, cash data will be used in the Accounting Domain. How this happens is akin to database security. Many may have read access to certain data in a corporate database for their own analyses, but you don't always want everyone to have write access and to change critical data that affect others. The Accounting Domain should have read access to cash data while OC Domain should have write access too, because that is where the data are being created. Likewise, improvement opportunities should be modeled in the OC Domain to capture operations and cash improvements as is documented in Chapter 17.

Improving Efficiency

We tend to believe that becoming more efficient when using capacity saves money. If we save time or increase output, we reduce costs. Let's consider the $30 laborer. Assume she can create 15 units of output per hour. Now, let's increase the amount of output to 20 then 25 then, ultimately, 30. What you will see in the Accounting Domain is that the cost per unit output decreases. It starts at $2 (15 units when using average costing where the cost is divided by output), moves to $1.50 (20 units), to $1.2 (25 units) to a final of $1 (30 units). What has happened is that you have moved down the same isocash curve as a result of being more efficient. The cost per unit may have decreased, but you've still spent $30 (Exhibit 8.1).

I often get the response, "Yeah, but I can sell more." Can you? First, not all work output is salable. How do you sell a processed AP invoice, or an interview HR has, unless that is the business you're in? Second, if the output is salable, the argument assumes there is demand for what is being

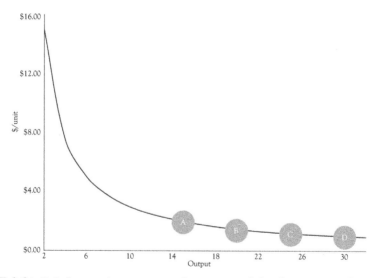

Exhibit 8.1 Increasing output at the same cash level moves you down the isocash curve. Hence, while the cost per unit is lower in the Accounting Domain, the cash cost remains unchanged

sold. There may not be. Finally, if it's sold, that's a revenue increase, not a cost decrease.

As we will see and as Toyota experienced, by focusing on the means, being efficient helps you meet demand by spending less money.

Isocash Shifts

The only way to reduce $cash_{OUT}$ from a capacity perspective is to buy less or cheaper input. This can be illustrated by considering isocash curves. As you move along a single isocash curve, you are not changing $cash_{OUT}$ and, hence, $cost_C$. You are changing $cost_{NC}$ which isn't money by definition. To save money, you must shift to a lower isocash curve, where you will be spending less money. You can do this two ways. The first is by buying cheaper capacity; think of paying $25 versus $30 for an hour of labor. The second is buying less capacity; think of buying six versus eight hours of labor. In both cases, you will shift to a lower isocash curve, which will be reflected, cash-wise, as a lower $cash_{OUT}$.

Reducing Costs

When reducing costs, the emphasis should be on reducing $cash_{OUT}$, the rate cash leaves your firm. As suggested previously, this comes primarily from managing capacity and knowing how you're moving on, and between isocash curves. The two situations mentioned next illustrate how to use efficiency improvements and isocash curves to reduce $cash_{OUT}$. They are, to a limited extent, managing the means.

Situation 1

Let's say you have three people doing a job and your company is in cost reduction mode. Each person can process five units of output per hour. Let's say you lean the operation and now each person can now process eight units of output per hour. If demand is for 15, you now have the ability to meet that demand with less capacity; two versus three people. This positions you to buy less capacity and put yourself on a lower isocash curve (Exhibit 8.2).

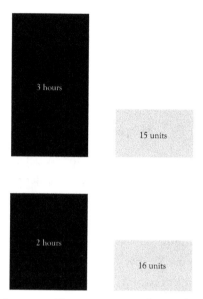

Exhibit 8.2 Efficiency enables you to meet demand using less input

Situation 2

Now you're in growth mode. You have the same three associates process-ing five units of output each. Once you exceed a demand of 15 units, you would need at least one more person. Every time you increase demand to a multiple of 5 or greater, you will need to hire another person. Now, let's say you lean the process so they're achieving eight per hour. Now you can hire based on multiples of eight. In the pre lean scenario, 40 units of output would require eight employees. In the post lean scenario, you just need five. The amount of cash required to meet demand should be less if you're efficient and you take advantage of it by buying less capacity.

Being more efficient will not reduce cash costs. The cash cost, $cost_C$, function increases monotonically, suggesting the more you do, the cost will stay the same or increase, but it will not decrease. Efficiency enables improvements to occur. First, although your costs won't go down, they will increase more slowly when managed effectively. Second, it creates options with respect to how much capacity you need to buy. Toyota could spend less, relatively speaking, because it did not need to buy excessive capacity to hide inefficiencies.

CHAPTER 9

BDM Cash Dynamics Framework

Earlier in the book, I described the anatomy of cash transactions. The idea of describing it this way came to me when I was in graduate school trying to figure out what was wrong with the accounting treatment of costs as it related to cash. It started with a particular analysis approach well known to engineers.

I'm a degreed engineer, so the approach I used wasn't just tattooed into my thought process, it was beaten in so hard, it has become a part of my DNA. The basic idea is this. If we're lost or stuck, we go back to first principles; foundational ideas we believe to be true. In this case, as a mechanical engineer, I thought about thermodynamics. Thermodynamics is one of those courses that you either understood, or you're beyond lost. I'll admit, when I first took thermo as an undergraduate, I had no clue what some of the terms meant when thinking of them in the physical versus theoretical/mathematical world. There is enthalpy, entropy, adiabatic, and many other complicated terms that, in some cases, described relatively simple ideas, but came across as being extremely complicated. But the one thing I did understand completely was the notion of a control volume. A control volume is a box you put around what you want to analyze or study and watch what comes into and leaves the box over a given period of time. It doesn't get much easier to understand than that!

My objective, in this case, was to analyze a company making money, so I used my extensive knowledge of thermodynamics to draw a box around a company. What next? I needed a way to describe what was happening from a cash perspective. Thermodynamics could do this, but the explanations seemed too complex; remember adiabatic, and isothermal. I then turned to system dynamics.

Bingo. System dynamics is a concept created at MIT by Jay Forrester. The idea was to find a way to model systems using engineering tools and concepts. According to Forrester, a system is "a grouping of parts that operate together for a common purpose."[1] The concept of system dynamics has been applied successfully in many areas, such as modeling business dynamics and cycles, populations, and even socioeconomic systems.

One key concept of system dynamics modeling is the level. The level is what we call a state variable. State variables describe the state of a system at any given time. If you studied animals in the wild, for instance, the population of a species or the amount of food sources could be considered state variables and would tell you something about the state of the population system. It would tell you how many of a given species there are, or how much food is available to them in the system you're studying and ultimately describe or project a system's dynamics or how it may change over time. For example, an abundance of food as a state variable may lead to increases in another state variable, the population we are interested in studying. An abundance of predators may lead to a reduced population, which may cause the food of the population we are studying to become abundant.

Cash, in this case, seemed to be a good candidate to be a level for a company, and so it became one in the analysis. If you draw a box around a company and watch the cash that comes in and leaves, you can garner a significant amount of information about cash levels, flow, and whether you're making or losing money (Exhibit 9.1).

With the box around the company, certain analyses are simplified. For instance, you can determine how much cash you have at any time by considering how much you started with and what came in and left the box during the analysis period as stated in Equation 2.1. For instance, your company starts the year with $1M, receives $1M throughout the year and spends $1.2M. At the end of the year, it has $800K. I start my day with $20, I make $2, and give my wife $22. At the end of the day, I'm broke again. This is straight from Equation 2.1.

$$\text{Cash}_{\text{FINAL}} = \text{Cash}_{\text{INITIAL}} + \Sigma\text{Cash}_{\text{IN}} - \Sigma\text{Cash}_{\text{OUT}} \qquad (9.1)$$

---

[1] Forrester, J.W. 1990. *Principles of Systems*, 1–1, Portland, OR: Productivity Press.

Exhibit 9.1 *Putting a box around the company and measuring cash$_{IN}$ and cash$_{OUT}$ provides, arguably, the most effective way to model cash over a period. This process also helps focus you on what does, and does not affect cash in ways cost accounting can not*

Critical to the analysis is to start with the box. If you read my first book, *Explicit Cost Dynamics*, the box around the company was the cost-revenue or CR Border. It has now been renamed the Cash$_{IN}$ Cash$_{OUT}$ or CICO Border. You then measure what comes in and what leaves during the analysis period. Understanding the flow in and out isn't enough when it comes to managing cash, however. One can argue cash flow statements can try to provide this info. We understand from this analysis and cash flow statements *that* cash flows but not *why* it flows. To understand this, we go back to the Business Operations Framework. To understand why and when money comes in and the rate or extent to which it does, we look to what we sold and our payment terms. To understand the flow out of the company and the extent to which it does, you look at what was bought and paid for; capacity, transactions, and TF&R.

This falls right in line with the activities of the Business Operations Framework. When you combine the Business Operations Framework with the Cash Flow Dynamics Framework, you end up with the OC Domain; the 3-D ball. Everything there is to know about the company and its performance, both operationally and financially exists, or is derived from OC Domain data. You know what was sold and what revenue was received versus recognized. You know what was brought in and spent. From this, you know if you're making money. You know how much capacity you bought, how much was consumed, and how this turned into output. You have practically everything you want to know. However, that one person will raise their hand and ask, "Yes, but what did the output cost?"

CHAPTER 10

Problem—The Process of Calculating Costs

We're on a roll, humming along. Everything is fine because we have all the information we want and need to manage operations and cash. The goal of the company is to make money, and we have an analysis that helps us understand how much we have at any given time, whether we are making money, the extent to which we are, and the levers that allow us to improve how much we can make. We know how much capacity we bought, how we consumed or used it to create the output and how efficiently, effectively, and productively we've done so. We also know what we've sold and collected. We can calculate practically any key managerial metric, cleanly, from these data. But when someone asks, "What did the output cost?" all hell breaks loose. The question is, "Why does it break loose?"

Before diving in, I'd like to share an idea we can use as context. I have used the terms data and information to represent numbers, measures, and metrics. I once heard an excellent way to distinguish between data and information; data are the raw numbers, and information is the answer to a question. The answer, information, comes from processing the data via an analysis or transformation of some sort. With the OC Domain, we have all the data the company creates available to us. However, when someone asks, "What did it cost?" the answer doesn't exist as native OC Domain data. Instead, the data involved in answering the question have to be processed, transformed into a different format to create a cost.

Consider the following example. You have a worker whom you pay $240 for eight hours for her time. This is based on a $30 per hour wage rate. She performs a task that takes 1.5 hours. These are all OC Domain data. What did the task cost? One simple way is to take the OC Domain data and suggest that since each hour "costs" $30, 1.5 hours would cost

$45. Notice, there is no cash transaction for $45 that leaves the company when she performs the task. The answer is a calculated cost that exists outside the OC Domain.

There is an anatomy to calculating costs (Exhibit 10.1). All business data, whether operational or financial, are created in the OC Domain. To answer the question about the task cost, we take a subset of the data, $30 per hour and the 1.5 hours to complete the task, to create our scope in this case. We then transform this into a cost by multiplying the two. This transformation creates an image or a projection of the OC Domain data, a cost of $45. (Exhibit 10.2). This image is like the circle created by projecting the 3-D ball in 2-D table.

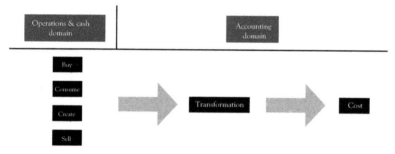

Exhibit 10.1 *The anatomy of a cost transformation begins with the OC Domain data. A set of this data is selected as the scope and, through an allocation/assignment schema, transformed into an Accounting Domain cost*

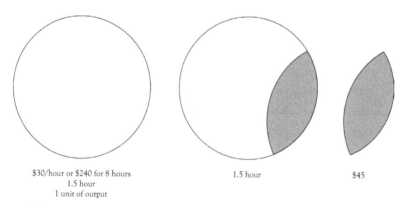

Exhibit 10.2 *In one case, we can look at the data and transform the data into a $45 cost*

What is this image? It's not money. $45 isn't spent when she performs the task and $45 isn't saved if she doesn't. I would argue it is an opinion of the value placed on the consumption of capacity. The $45 value reflects 1.5 hours at an assumed value of $30 per hour. Recall, there is no math relationship between the capacity you buy and how it is used. To calculate a cost, you need a relationship. When you need a relationship and don't have one, you make one up. In this case, I assumed every hour was worth $30, so 1.5 of them must be worth $45. It we had paid an outsider $45 for the same output, money would have crossed the CICO Border meaning it would have been a cash cost, $cost_C$. However, since no money left the company when the work was performed internally, it is a non-cash cost, or $cost_{NC}$.

When we ask most questions, we often expect a unique answer. For instance, if we ask what time it is, we expect 3:00 PM, not "it's either 1:45 PM, 3:00 PM, or 4:17 AM." When we weigh ourselves, we expect 150 lbs., not 110, 150, or 165. We'd prefer to be told the widget costs $1.28 to make, rather than it could cost $1.28, or 99¢ or $2.79. When we ask what something costs, we *should* expect a unique value; it costs $7.35. With measured values, you can converge on a unique value. However, the calculated cost of a product, service, or activity is $cost_{NC}$, and it is not a unique value because there is no single way to calculate it.

Consider, for instance, a different allocation schema. Say, over the entire shift, she performs the task five times. If the scope is the entire shift, the total amount of money spent is $240. If we divide by five tasks, we end up with a $cost_{NC}$ of $48 per task. Now, what if only seven of the eight hours purchased are productive. If we want to focus on productive time, we're looking at $210 versus $240. If we divide the $210 by five, we now have a cost of $42 per task. Again, no new data are created, as all data were created and available in the OC Domain before the cost calculation. Instead, how we choose, subjectively, to project a past event or set of events, created the answer. We considered a different scope; one shift or a partial shift. We also considered a different allocation or assignment schema—time to create versus number created. Each choice created a new cost. This process is demonstrated in Exhibit 10.3. The cost can also be affected by allocation/assignment schemata.

This resulting image is your calculated cost. It is information derived from OC Domain data and transformed to create accounting information (Exhibit 10.3).

There are a number of inherent problems with this process. First, the numbers are not unique. For every calculated cost you believe to be true, accurate, or precise, someone else with a different scope or allocation schema can create a different value. Neither yours nor the other is right because, recall, the scope is subjective, and the allocation is arbitrary. Hence, regardless of the approach, the number will not be unique or represent cash. Some ask if better allocation schemata model cash more effectively. For instance, is activity-based costing better than lean accounting or standard costing? The answer is, "No." Costing methodologies can't partially represent cash just like a woman can't be partially pregnant. You are either pregnant or you aren't; you either model cash or you don't. Costing models do not.

Second, while all of the gyrations are being made to calculate a cost in the Accounting Domain, nothing has changed in the OC Domain. The OC Domain is the source of your unique data, and it is devoid of subjective and arbitrary treatments of data. Thus, it is the OC Domain where operations and cash-based analyses should begin and remain. Only when reporting information is required should the OC Domain data be transferred into Accounting Domain information.

This suggests one final idea. You do not need calculate costs for managerial purposes. The data in the OC Domain are precise and unambiguous. The Accounting Domain information is ambiguous and messy. I describe OC Domain data as tomatoes, garlic, basil, and onions while calculated costs are store-bought spaghetti sauce. It may have some of the important raw ingredients, but it also has a lot of the other additives that we may or may not know or understand, and in the end, they are less healthy for you.

Let's delve more deeply into the Accounting Domain.

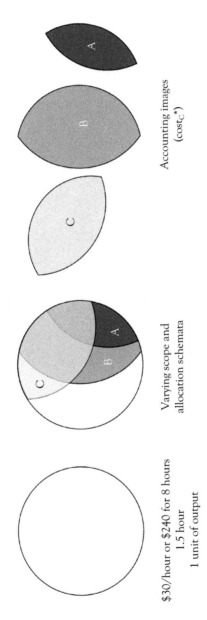

$30/hour or $240 for 8 hours
1.5 hour
1 unit of output

Varying scope and
allocation schemata

Accounting images
(cost_C^*)

Exhibit 10.3 Different ways of looking at the situation in the OC Domain will lead to unique images or costs

CHAPTER 11

The Accounting Domain

For all the good things the OC Domain can do, there are still several things it cannot do. Recall, the OC Domain was designed to model operations and cash. It is incapable of calculating costs, assessing the value of assets such as inventory, or handling accruals and matching. Many of these may be required for reporting purposes, which suggests, the OC Domain and its raw data are not suitable for corporate reporting.

I believe the Accounting Domain exists for two reasons. First is reporting corporate performance. Governments have rules and regulations by which companies must abide. In the United States, companies file income statements, balance sheets, and statements of cash flow. There are certain rules related to how each is created and sometimes, these rules violate what happens in the OC Domain. For instance, the income statement may use calculated costs and matching to calculate gross margins. Both violate the cash dynamics from the OC Domain. Depreciation and amortization, too, are accounting concepts that do not exist, and have no meaning, in the OC Domain. When considering the balance sheet, inventory value, for instance, is not something that can be determined in the OC Domain. Inventory value uses concepts related to calculating costs; hence, it, too, does not reflect cash and is not a unique value. Finally, with the indirect method of creating cash flow statements, non-cash information may be taken from the income statement and balance sheet, both of which have accruals-based information, which compromises the cash integrity of the statements. This, of course, renders the OC Domain from even creating certain types of cash flow statements.

The second purpose of the Accounting Domain is to answer managerial questions that only accounting can answer, such as "What does this product (service, or activity) cost?" or "What is the gross margin of a particular product or service?" Answers to questions such as these require a transformation of OC Domain data into the Accounting Domain.

That the Accounting Domain can do the latter does not add validity to the practice of asking such questions. Drawing mythological figures does not bring them to life. As discussed last chapter, costs and, therefore margins, are not unique. They are subjected to the scope and assignment schema chosen. Therefore, if someone asks you what something costs, the answer is an opinion of the value of consumed capacity, not money. It should not be considered as $cost_C$, and decisions based on the assumption it is money should be avoided at all costs.

CHAPTER 12

From OC Domain to Accounting Domain

Accounting information begins as OC Domain data. Let's revisit our worker being paid $30 per hour for an eight hour day. She's switched from phone calls to widgets. Cross training. Now, let's say you consumed seven of her eight hours making widgets. In that seven hours of productive time, she makes 56 widgets.

The OC Domain data suggests you paid $240 for eight hours of work. Seven of the eight hours was used to create the 56 widgets. Now, someone asks an Accounting Domain question; "What does a widget cost to create?" The simplest approach would be to take the $240 and divide it by the number of units created, 56 for a unit cost of $4.29. Now someone comes along and suggests this calculation may not be accurate. Might it be a more accurate reflection of production costs to only use productive time? Instead of using the full eight hours which may include lunch, bathroom breaks, or goofing off time, only focus on the seven hours of production time. In this case, the cost per unit would be $3.75. Note, as described in Chapter 10, by changing the scope from eight hours to seven hours, the cost per unit has gone from $4.29 to $3.75 all based on a choice that was made regarding the transformation of OC Domain data into Accounting Domain information (Exhibit 12.1).

There are a few things to note about accounting costs. First, as is demonstrated in the example, choices can be made in the transformation to the Account Domain that affect the cost image created. In this case, by changing the scope from eight hours to seven, the cost went down 54¢. This is pretty substantial, relatively speaking, and the impact could be just as substantial. Say someone offered you $4 for each widget. Would you take it? In one case, you'd feel you were making money ($3.75 cost) and in the other, you'd feel you were losing money ($4.29). When looking at

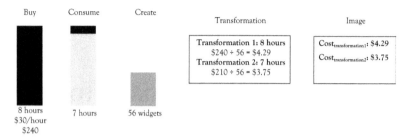

Exhibit 12.1 *Different costs can be calculated by changing assumptions. Knowing this is key when dealing with calculated cost information*

OC Domain data, you would make $224 and spend $240 regardless of scope and the transformation algorithm. However, in the first case, you may turn away $224 in cash and have nothing, leaving you $240 in the hole. Or, you would get the full $224 and only be in the hole $16. The $224 would cover 93 percent of the salary you'd have to pay the worker, because she was paid regardless of what she made and was sold. While the scenario changes in the Accounting Domain, it remains unperturbed and, therefore, unchanged in the OC Domain (Exhibit 12.2). This suggests there is value in understanding the real, unprocessed data coming from the OC Domain and making managerial decisions based on these data rather than Accounting Domain information.

Second, the Accounting Domain creates information that is dangerous to the untrained eye. The problem is, most eyes, in this context, are untrained. Let's assume we create a curve of possible costs for widgets. We start with $240 and divide it by the number of widgets, creating an isocash curve. The isocash curve suggests the cost per unit goes down with more output. For instance, the cost per unit for 56 units is $4.29. The cost per unit for 60 units is $4. At 52 units, the cost per unit is $4.62. Notice, by going from 52 to 56 units, the cost difference is 33¢ while going from 56 to 60 units, the same four unit increase, the difference is 29¢. Two questions. The first is, what does the decreasing cost represent monetarily? Remember, cash cost functions increase monotonically, so what does it mean that costs actually go down with more output? The second question is, what does it imply when going from 52 to 56 units has a greater impact than going from 56 to 60? And recall, we're dealing with the same

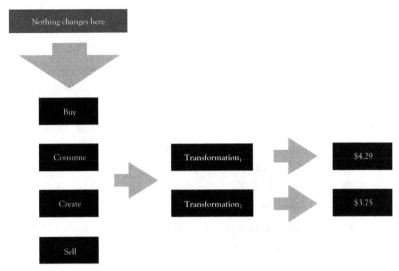

Exhibit 12.2 **When accounting transformations occur, they happen in the Accounting Domain. None of the data from the OC Domain changes as a result of the transformation**

$cost_C$, $240, so nothing has changed from a cash perspective. This also suggests you will increase your margins by increasing output. While the calculation is correct in the Accounting Domain, the OC Domain suggests you haven't spent any less money, so you haven't saved money.

Many believe moving along this isocash curve has true cost-based monetary value. It doesn't. Moving from one point to the other has significance in the Accounting Domain because the calculated cost, $cost_{NC}$, changes. However, as long as you're on the $240 isocash curve, the amount of money spent has not changed. The only way costs change from a cash perspective is to jump to a lower isocash curve.

Not understanding isocash curves can create confusion and cause smart people to make bad choices and decisions. For instance, consider the customer mentioned earlier that was focused on cost per unit without considering the isocash curve they were on. They believed being at a more cost efficient point on a higher isocash curve with a lower cost per unit, was better than being at a less efficient point on a lower isocash curve. Or the customer that thought increasing gross margins would improve cash. Let's revisit the scenarios in a bit more detail.

Scenario 1

The first company would buy their products from a supplier that used an older, mass production technology. Their supplier produced in large batches and sold their products at a lower unit price to my customer. Let's say the customer would buy 10,000 units at a time for $10,000. In the Accounting Domain, they calculated this to be $1 per unit. In the OC Domain, they spent $10,000 to buy 10,000 units. Note the difference.

I suggested they consider buying a newer, smaller batch technology. With this approach, 5,000 units could be purchased for $8,000. In the Accounting Domain, the common assumption is that they would be worse off because the cost per unit *increased* to $1.60 from $1. They would lose 60¢ on each unit when buying the smaller batch technology, right? Although true in the Accounting Domain, the OC Domain suggested they pay $8000 for 5,000 units. When factoring in demand, which rarely exceeded 5,000 for each product, the answer was very different. Selling 5,000 units, the revenue was set. Say each unit sold for $10 for a revenue cap of $50,000. The OC Domain suggested the company could either spend $10,000 to make $50,000 or they could spend $8,000 to make $50,000. Given the options presented like this, which would you choose? The Accounting Domain suggested they would lose money by going with the more expensive technology. The OC Domain suggested they would make more money by going with the solution that was calculated to be less profitable in the Accounting Domain.

Scenario 2

This customer looked to increase their gross margins by becoming more efficient. Assume the sales price for their product was $5. The units were made by laborers who made $15 per hour. The laborers typically produced 30 units per hour. In the Accounting Domain, one possible image is 50¢ per unit. This results in a gross margin of $4.50 ignoring all other factors. The company implements a lean program and now the laborer can make 40 versus 30 units. They are still being paid the same, $15 per hour cash$_{OUT}$. Now, the unit cost has moved down the isocash curve to 38¢ per unit. This has increased gross margins by 12¢ per unit, right?

Well, yes, in the Accounting Domain. However, the OC Domain sees the scenario differently. In the OC Domain, *costs have gone up*. Why? Revenue is the same; $cash_{IN}$ for each item doesn't change. Labor pay is the same, so $cash_{OUT}$ doesn't change from a labor cost perspective. But now, because you're reporting a higher unit margin in the Accounting Domain, the taxes will increase on each unit, so more money will leave the company.

The OC Domain data focuses you on what really happens when working with unambiguous data. In the first case, the OC Domain explanation is that the company would spend $2,000 in cash to increase their gross margin. Had this company been a for-profit company, this $2,000 would have also caused them to incur higher taxes; a double whammy. Additionally, they would end up with excess inventory. This excess inventory would go onto the balance sheet as an asset, but the implication is significant. The impact of exceeding demand is softened, if not encouraged, with a focus on gross margins in the Accounting Domain. The impact may be interpreted as a variance rather than spending an extra $2,000. In the second case, the company changed nothing cash-wise, but by blindly focusing on Accounting Domain information, they lost money.

Let's go back to the notion of how the Accounting Domain came about, what it is, and what it does. The Accounting Domain is for reporting OC Domain activities based on certain techniques, rules, and regulations. It creates projections, each, one of practically an infinite number of possible projections, of what happened in the OC Domain. It doesn't add anything new. There are no new data, just information, and a projection, based on opinion, rules, and regulations.

CHAPTER 13

Costs and Profit: What's in a Name?

I eat meat. This may offend some, but I do. If I offend you by doing so, I apologize. One of my favorite meats is steak. I love steak. Someone mentioning a steak dinner conjures up various images for steak lovers. For some, steak may mean Outback. For others, it may mean Morton's. Steak from Outback is different from steak served at Morton's. Not to knock either one, they're just different. The same word, steak, has two interpretations. Hence, when talking about steak, using the right language and setting the most appropriate context is important. If you ask someone to go have a steak and you take them to the restaurant they were not thinking about, there may be a good amount of surprise, but there may also be disappointment, especially if you're at Morton's expecting Outback prices.

The same thing happens in business. We speak in terms of costs or profit, but what we often miss is that although the words are the same, cost and profit, they mean very different things when in the OC Domain versus the Accounting Domain. If you are talking about one and you mean the other, confusion, surprise, and even disappointment may ensue. Let's compare costs and profits across domains.

In the OC Domain, a cost is money spent, $cost_C$. There is a clear and concise cash transaction; money for something, where that something is usually either capacity or services. Its value and timing directly influence $cash_{OUT}$.

To figure out a cost, you look at what you bought or are obliged to pay, how much you have to pay, and when it leaves your firm. Compare this to calculated accounting costs. To figure out a cost, you must take OC Domain data and process them using one of the millions of combinations of scope and assignment schema available to transform the data.

Think about the number of assumptions and approaches you can use to calculate the cost of a local call. Should you use 24 hours for 30 days? Some months have 31, 28, or even 29 days. Does the cost of a call change based on the number of days in the month? You're generally not making calls if you're not working, so how long is your work day? Include bathroom and food breaks? Do you include all calls or only those tied to that being costed? As you can see, there are so many ways to calculate a cost, suggesting a high level of subjectivity.

The two costs represent very different things. $cost_C$ only represents cash that leaves the firm. Calculated costs, $cost_{NC}$, represent an option of value. When speaking of costs, it is important to highlight the difference by acknowledging whether you're talking about $cost_C$ or $cost_{NC}$. If you are focused on cost reductions and the value you're focused on is $cost_{NC}$, you may see cost reductions with no money being saved.

A funny anecdote that highlights this comes from a friend who once shared a story that made no sense to me. Back when Bill Gates was actively working for Microsoft, the friend told me if Bill Gates bent over to pick up a $100 bill, he would lose money. He actually believed this. His logic was based on breaking down Bill Gates's salary to a per second basis, and argued he made more than he would in the 2 seconds it would take Bill to pick up the $100. This is clearly nonsense for several reasons, however, there are several examples in business where similar decisions are made. The construction project manager who doesn't consider the difference between internal labor and contracted labor, or renting equipment versus using that which her company owns. Or the hospital executive who thinks it actually costs the hospital $7000 per day for a patient to be admitted.

The same thing happens with profit. There is profit in the Accounting Domain. This value is not money. As mentioned previously, gross profit includes non-cash values such as COGS, and may be subjected to matching which violates the laws of cash flow. Then there is cash profit, or offset, which is an OC Domain value that considers $cash_{IN}$ versus $cash_{OUT}$ over a period. As with costs, it is important to know which you're talking about. You can increase cash profit without affecting accounting profit, and you can even have situations where the accounting profit can increase while cash profit decreases.

Language, therefore, is very important when speaking in the context of a two-domain framework. If the focus is on cost reduction, ask yourself "which cost?" The answer is often "both," so you will want governing principles to decide which one trumps the other. Are you more interested in generating cash profit or accounting profit? Companies sometimes struggle with the notion that reducing accounting costs may increase cash costs, and this has an effect when searching for the right answer and the actions to support it. If the focus is solely on making money, cash should win.

PART III

The Execution

CHAPTER 14

Business Cash Modeling, Management, and Projection

Execution starts by focusing on cash. Notionally, since cash is the most important factor, all else exists to help us model and understand cash. When I speak to people in finance functions, I am amazed at how difficult two concepts they seem to struggle with are; understanding how much money they're making and spending, and modeling and projecting cash. Well, perhaps not amazed, but certainly nonplussed by the notion they're so difficult. There are aspects of cash modeling that are more difficult than others, namely estimating revenues coming in. Timing and amount of revenues projected to come are often difficult for companies in many business industry sectors. Beyond that, it is pretty straightforward. So, why the difficulty?

I believe companies and finance/accounting types struggle with cash and projecting cash flow because they are trying to do so in the Accounting Domain where information has been created through the transformation of OC Domain data rather in the OC Domain where cash and the factors that affect cash reside in their native format. This creates confusion because they are trying to project cash using non-cash data. Additionally, accruals throw off the timing of when cash actually flows.

With this chapter, I will demonstrate the techniques I use for cash modeling that shift focus away from the Accounting Domain and helps create significantly more clarity. It isn't only straightforward, it is also insightful. Most of the unique perspectives I've been involved with creating, developing, and implementing have come directly from this approach and what it tells me both mathematically and business wise. Here are the four steps:

1. Commit to the model
2. Build the model using the $Cash_{IN}$-$Cash_{OUT}$ Border

3. Creating business cash requirements (BCR)
4. Calculating offset

Step 1: Committing to the Model

The first step is probably the most difficult for most people. We are inundated with Accounting Domain concepts and information in everyday life. When we're shopping, we are shown cost per kilogram, for instance, and we use that for comparisons; which product is the cheapest per kilogram? My wife is famous in our house for doing it. I say so lovingly, of course. She may buy a six pack of water for $3 and proudly say, "This costs 50 cents per bottle." This is not true, however. If she assembled six individual bottles of water at a price of 50 cents per bottle, then she bought them at 50 cents per bottle. Instead, she brought an unbreakable six pack for $3.

You may ask, what's the difference? What's the big deal? The big deal is this. First, it can mislead you when you are in decision making mode. This especially happens when it comes to volume buying, where the idea something is cheaper per bottle may be an incentive to buy more than there is demand for. Six for $3 certainly sounds like a better deal than three for $2, so we may buy the six because we felt we found a great deal. Demand is not a part of that buying calculus.

Instead of this, what I typically propose is the notion of the *cost to meet demand*. If demand is for six bottles and you pay $3, it is the same, cash wise, as buying six bottles for 50 cents each. It is more expensive than buying six bottles for 49¢ and less expensive than six bottles for 51¢. The difference is subtle, but from a managerial perspective, it is significant. The question shifts to, "What is the least amount I can spend to get what I really need or to meet the demand of the market?" In the earlier example, it is cheaper to buy three for $2 than six for $3 if the demand is for three or fewer bottles. You are spending $2 versus $3 to meet the demand.

Another challenge I encounter with business folks is, they attempt to operate in a mixed domain environment, which was brought up in Chapter 5. Mixed domain means all costs and profits are the same because there is no separation, in their minds, between the OC Domain and the

Accounting Domain. As I speak to them about different domains, the question I often bring up to set expectations and focus effort is, "Do you want to make accounting profit, or do you want to make money, cash profit?" Their response is often, we're all about that cash! Making money! Then they start talking about making money in the context of gross margins, which is squarely in the Accounting Domain. "If my costs are $4 and my revenues are $3.95, we're losing money." I respond, "Well, that's an accounting representation, not a cash transaction, but we've been led to believe it's cash. We've been bamboozled." They respond, "I get that, but I need a robust costing model to determine my costs more accurately, so I know if I made money, blah, blah, blah."

The key is this. If you want to focus on cash, you must focus on the OC Domain and leave the Accounting Domain to reporting as described in Chapter 11. The reasons for this are:

1. Accounting Domain adds no new data. All Accounting Domain information comes from OC Domain data, so all the data you need resides in the OC Domain.
2. Accounting Domain converts some $cost_C$ costs to $cost_{NC}$ information. When you take a laborer making $30 per hour and convert it to $4.85 per part, you're no longer dealing with cash.
3. All cash costs occur in the OC Domain, not the Accounting Domain. Recall, cash costs result from capacity, transactions, and taxes, fees, and royalties, all of which reside in the OC Domain.

Committing to the model means OC Domain questions and analyses remain in the OC Domain. Likewise, accounting analyses should focus on reporting and remain in the Accounting Domain. In this context, there is no confusion or ambiguity. When someone talks about cost reduction, you should ask to clarify, "Are you talking about $cost_C$ reductions or $cost_{NC}$ reductions?" When they talk about profit, ask if they're talking about cash profit in the OC Domain, or accounting profit in the Accounting Domain. If they cannot answer or distinguish, they are in mixed domain mode and simplification and clear communication will be more challenging but necessary.

Step 2: The $Cash_{IN}$-$Cash_{OUT}$ (CICO) Border

The next step is to build the model itself. This process starts with defining the parameters or scope of the analysis. There is a clear answer to this. Use the CICO Border. Anything that comes into the box (company) in the context of receiving money through this box is cash revenue. Anything that leaves in the form of payments is a cost, specifically $cost_C$. This border is very important for a number of reasons. First, it establishes the foundation for the cash profit equation. The cash you have at the end of a period is equal to what you started with, plus what came in through the period, minus what left through the same period. Very clear and unambiguous. Second, and equally unambiguous, is defining the terms of revenue and costs. Consider revenue. You either received money from a sale or you didn't. Unlike revenue recognition in the Accounting Domain, if you don't have the money, it isn't revenue and, therefore, doesn't impact cash. Think, too, about cost reductions. If costs are reduced, the rate of $cash_{OUT}$ should be less; you are spending less money to meet demand.

The CICO Border must go around the entire company and not just a department or a division. When you put the box around a division, you create the opportunity for misleading data and information, and to support bad decisions that appear justified. With misleading data and information, you create the opportunity to do things such as suggest budget transfers are departmental or divisional revenue. They are not revenue opportunities for the company. Paying IT to unjam your printer from your budget is neither a cost to the firm nor is it revenue to the firm resulting from a payment to IT. It's like a wife giving her husband money. She has less in her pocket and he has more in his, but in the end, the couple has the same amount of money.

One of the worst abuses of this is the notion of profit centers. With profit centers, the department or group has prices for the products or services they offer. The idea is to operate at a profit, where the revenues they receive are greater than their "cost" to operate. I get what they're trying to do but think about this. Let's say you have a shared services center composed primarily of capacity and is deemed a profit center with a "cost" of $20. Another group within the same company uses the services of this profit center. However, since the shared services center must show a profit, it charges 1.2 • $20 or $24 for its services to this other group. The second group has "costs" of $50 before considering the costs of the shared services group. They sell themselves to someone else, again within the company. What do they use as their total cost? $74. But if they, too, are a profit center and they need to show a profit, they may charge 1.2 • $74 or $88.80 to someone on the outside looking to buy their service. You see where this is going. The organization cost is $70. However, this group thinks its cost is $74. It now believes to get a 20 percent markup, it must sell the opportunity for $88.80. $84 would have given them the 20 percent return on cash, but now, with the artificially inflated costs, they potentially price themselves out of the market. If someone offered $85, they may turn down the offer!

My favorite example of this was in a previous life as a professor. The school decided to charge for a shared services copy center. Say, for simplicity, they charged five cents per copy. With a box around my department, it made sense to pay a group outside the college, three cents per copy. The college, by choosing to charge for use of its own resources, created an incentive to increase spending and therefore, costs. How? The school still paid for the copy center, so the $cash_{OUT}$ was basically the same. However, by paying an external group for the same service, more cash passed the CICO Border to pay the outside service provider, leading to higher cash expenditures.

Once the parameters are established, the modeling is pretty straightforward. You pick an analysis period, create your foundational data model, and analyze $cash_{IN}$ and $cash_{OUT}$.

Step 3: Business Cash Requirements

Business cash requirements, or BCR, is the foundation of cash profit management, and is one of the most important cash values there is. BCR tells you what the company is spending and has spent both during the period and cumulatively. Your cash model is simply inflows and outflows ($cash_{IN}$ and $cash_{OUT}$) of cash. BCR is the sum of all $cash_{OUT}$. By adding all $cash_{OUT}$, you can create an understanding of the periodic cash requirements of the company and use this to project how cash will change over time.

When we look at outflows of cash, there are three components that become critical. The three are:

- Taxes, Fees, and Royalties
- Transactions
- Capacity

The three are listed in this order on purpose. First, the top two are generally well understood and analyzed. People know they exist and have spent a good amount of time trying to manage them. The third, however, needs additional consideration and analysis.

I will address the first two in the context of the model quickly and will then focus on capacity the rest of the way.

Taxes, Fees, and Royalties (TF&R)

The cash dynamics of taxes are pretty straightforward. When it is time to pay them, they leave and deplete cash by the amount paid. What is important to note here is, taxes are determined not by what happens in the OC Domain, but by how the images projected into the Accounting Domain affect what was reported. As taxable income increases in the Accounting Domain, tax rates increase and vice versa. Factors such as depreciation, which falls clearly in the Accounting Domain, too, affects tax rate. These are ultimately determined by the transformation scope and allocation schema. With depreciation, the schedule doesn't align with cash payments for the equipment. Depending on the technique you use to depreciate the equipment, which is a transformation decision, your taxable income and, therefore, taxes will be affected. This, again, is independent of the cash transaction and payment terms tied to buying the equipment.

Fees and royalties are other forms of cash payments where nothing is bought, but payments are made. Examples are fines, commissions, and royalties, where payments that are outside of normal BCR components. Sometimes, these can be planned and projected, and other times, they may occur unexpectedly.

Transaction Costs

Transactions are one-off situations where companies may buy something such as services. Unlike capacity where it is bought in anticipation of use or demand, transactions are bought to address specific issues. An example might be hiring a consultant to address a particular concern or hiring a grounds crew to manicure the corporate campus once per week.

The cash dynamics of transactions are straightforward like they were for TF&R. When you pay for the transaction, money leaves the firm. Managing the cash effect on BCR is a function of managing price, the amount you buy, and when you buy and pay for it.

Capacity

Like transaction costs cost dynamics of capacity are tied to how much you buy, how much you pay, and when you pay. The key difference is what the company "owns" or is responsible for. For instance, an IT department with dedicated employees is capacity and is "owned" figuratively, by the company. Bringing in Geek Squad to perform an install or repair would be a transaction. There are two reasons this is important to understand and distinguish. First, capacity is what the company pays for whether work is being performed or not. Imagine all work stops in your company. What will you still have to pay for? You'll still have rent, labor, equipment, and IT payments as well as any materials payments still due. This is mostly capacity, and it contributes to BCR. Whether money is coming into the firm or not, they must still be paid for. When you model these in the OC Domain, you will see predicable cash rates leaving the company to address these obligations.

The second reason this is important is, these data form the basis of management and planning activities. When you model current capacity levels, there is a cash component that comes along with it. This amount heavily influences BCR. If you have two offices, 35 employees, five pieces of equipment, and new servers you are paying for, you can calculate their cash costs both now, and into the future, so you know how much cash will be required by your largest expenditures and how long you will have to pay for them.

One of the key benefits of BCR is its instantaneous feedback as it relates to capacity. Say, for instance, you need to bring in a temporary worker for production or to help with salable services. From an Accounting Domain perspective, their cost would have to be transformed into the Accounting Domain based on the scope and chosen transformation algorithm. The result is that the cash required to pay for the worker would have to propagate through the transformation and either show up as a larger cost pool to be allocated or as a variance of some sort.

When modeling the cash implications of capacity, the effect is seen immediately without having to transform data or wait for it to propagate. You can see the immediate cash impact of hiring, laying off, or even overtime pay immediately, and when understanding capacity cash dynamics, you can project changes in cash requirements based on decisions regarding capacity levels (Exhibit 14.1). When you buy and pay for capacity, the impact is immediate. The $10,000 you paid for equipment is immediate

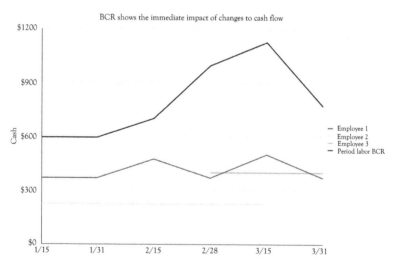

Exhibit 14.1 *This chart shows the individual BCR for three employees and the total BCR for each of several pay periods. Notice how you can see and predict the impact of things such as overtime (2/15), hiring (2/28) and firing (3/15) immediately. This can be critical when thinking about things such as planning overtime or workforce changes, especially for the small business. Compare this to looking at the impact as it relates to gross margins. None of this information is salient when looking at cost accounting information*

and salient, especially when compared to a $2,500 hit you may see on the income statement from depreciation.

Step 4: Offset

BCR establishes the cash payment requirements of your company. The key to making money is offsetting the BCR with revenue. Offset is a value that shows the rate of paying off BCR. Of course, this is done with money received.

Let's consider a simple example. Let's say your company spends $20,000 in capacity and related expenses monthly. Ultimately, you will need to receive at least $20,000 from cash$_{IN}$ on average every month to offset the BCR of $20,000. If you bring in $21,000, you have a positive offset of $1,000. If you bring in $18,000, you have a negative offset of $2,000.

Offset appears on the surface to be a fairly innocuous value. However, it is an extremely powerful value that places corporate cash in the context of whether you have made money more effectively than practically any other value. Consider a previous customer.

The customer was struggling to generate cash, so they brought my firm in. After analysis of the BCR versus offset, the problem became amazingly clear. Let's say the company's monthly BCR was $100,000. The company was only generating $60,000 in revenue, suggesting there was a negative offset of $40,000 each month. Everything they sold was profitable in the Accounting Domain, yet they had no money and were trending negatively at an increasing rate from a cash perspective, which is represented without using actual company data (Exhibit 14.2).

This firm, like most I deal with, both large and small, did not know whether they were making money or not. They *thought* they knew and thought they were. They could quote accounting metrics such as gross margins, net margins, EBITDA, and all sorts of other metrics, but the tools they used were all Accounting Domain metrics, which don't model cash. This perspective caused leaders and others to make decisions that may lead to positive accounting results and negative cash results.

When looking at BCR in the context of offset, one thing that becomes apparent is that the capacity costs, in general, do not go away until there is a specific action that causes them to be eliminated. Rent, for instance,

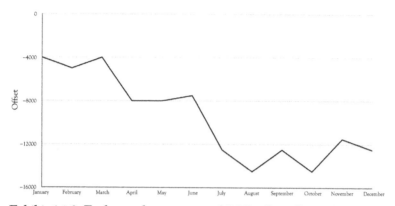

Exhibit 14.2 *Each month, revenue and BCR affect offset. This curve shows cumulative offset over a year. In September, the company was just over $12,000 away from breaking even for the year. In November, they had improved their position to being just under $12,000. Cumulative offset is an important value because 1. It provides a foundation for when and why you should you should adjust prices, and 2. How much money you need to generate to break even cash-wise*

exists for the length of the contract and the cash it consumes increases over time. This becomes a key consideration when focusing on making money, especially when it comes to pricing decisions. One example I like to consider was a time a few years back when I got an MRI on my shoulder.

Let's say the MRI cost was calculated to be $3,000. This would suggest the price should not go below $3,000. Let's look at this in the OC Domain.

In the OC Domain, very little changed as a function of my laying there in the machine. Consider the capacity costs. The machine costs were the same, the tech labor costs were the same, rent and staff costs were the same, and they had film in stock, so film didn't have to be purchased for me. The only factor that likely changed was utility costs, unless there was a "per use" clause in an equipment lease where money had to be paid each time an MRI was performed. In other words, the variable cash costs, $cost_C$, were relatively negligible.

When we think about what comprised the BCR, all the factors mentioned previously, labor, rent, film, equipment, staff, were values that would need to be paid for whether I was there or not. The objective, then, was to generate enough revenue to offset the BCR. From a cash perspective, as long as you know your BCR, you know how much revenue you need to offset to break-even from a cash perspective.

Now, someone asks, "How much does an MRI cost?" Hell breaks loose. To calculate this, portions of the capacity costs are captured and transformed into a calculated cost; $3,000. Again, this is $cost_{NC}$-a non-cash cost. They did not spend $3,000 as I laid there getting my MRI and they wouldn't have saved $3,000 had I not shown up. It is an opinion of the value of consumed capacity. However, when it comes to pricing, there is now a belief that the MRI must sell for at least $3,000 to make money. If someone came along and offered $2,500, the company would likely turn down the opportunity suggesting they would *lose* money. Recall, the cost could have been $2,500 or $3,500 just as easily as it was $3,000, and it's not money anyway.

The reality is that comparing money to $cost_{NC}$ makes no mathematical sense as discussed before. Pick-up trucks and trees. Hence, this notion of profitability analysis doesn't make sense mathematically either. However, the problem is deeper. Let's say, for the purpose of simplicity, the company has a monthly BCR of $1.3M. Now, $1.3M must be paid every month, whether the company is performing MRIs or not. If all someone is willing to pay is $2,500, that $2,500 is generating offset for the $1.3M that must be paid each month. By turning down the $2,500, the gap between what is paid out and how much is being offset will continue to grow as seen in Exhibit 14.2. Likewise, when you factor in price elasticity of demand, if you cannot sell enough MRIs at $3,000, each MRI you actually do sell may be profitable in the Accounting Domain, but they may not generate enough offset to break even from a cash perspective. If the objective is to make money, which one trumps? Profit or offset?

To manage cash, you have to model it effectively and you must have a governance approach to support cash-related decisions. The governance will help set priorities when conflict inevitably occurs. Understanding and managing cash is challenging if you are trying to do so from the Accounting Domain because that is non-cash accounting information not cash data.

The next chapter will take this one step further by looking at measures and metrics.

CHAPTER 15

BDM Measures and Metrics

The suggestion with BDM is that companies can, and in fact should, focus their managerial attention on the OC Domain. This includes both operational and financial analyses related to cash, cash flow, and managerial decisions. The data available in the OC Domain are tied to the source that created them and all data are unperturbed. Hence, they are operations and cash data in their native format. This makes them much easier to understand, interpret, and ultimately manage. For example, which is easier to comprehend and address? That you ran a $1.89 negative variance or that you made 18 units when the target was 20?

Since all business data are created in the OC Domain and are then transformed into the Accounting Domain when needed, moving your analyses into the OC Domain will not create a loss of data. Instead, there will be even more data. However, there may be a shift of information that may require you to update thinking in some areas. For instance, product and customer profitability do not exist in the OC Domain, and in this framework, the value of the numbers in the Accounting Domain is questionable. Instead, you would look at the revenue from the product or customer and compare that to the capacity consumed by that product or customer, and the offset generated.

This is really the same information as product and customer profitability without the drama. With customer profitability, the customer capacity consumption data are transformed by turning them into costs, which, of course, are Accounting Domain representations of OC Domain activities. The two hours spent trying to hunt down an order becomes a $150 cost for a customer. This creates drama because if you don't know this is $cost_{NC}$, you may compare it to revenue and draw conclusions regarding whether this affects how much money you've made from the customer.

If you drop clients that are unprofitable, you run the risk of losing the revenue and, therefore, offset while the BCR remains.

In the OC Domain, high maintenance customers consume more capacity. However, this has nothing to do with what you spent serving them and the amount of offset you generate from them. Recall, the capacity you buy and how you use it are independent. The company did not spend $150 in cash hunting down an order, so it did not lose $150 on the opportunity. Only time was lost. Thus, assigning capacity costs to a customer is a transformation. Looking at the reality of how much capacity a customer consumes is not. This paves the way to compare customers by looking at a customer efficiency metric such as revenue or offset generated compared to capacity consumed. If you have customers that consume more capacity, that doesn't mean you lose money or make less money with them. You can look for ways to reduce capacity consumption to make them more efficient by managing the means. But what should be clear is, if you eliminate unprofitable or inefficient customers or products without changing cash$_{OUT}$, you will lose money because the BCR remains the same, but you now generate less offset.

There are several metrics considered in the OC Domain that are important from a managerial perspective and can replace classic Accounting Domain metrics. Table 15.1 shows a few key metrics broken down by OC Domain categories. These will help you shift your analyses into the OC Domain without concern for a loss of data.

Table 15.1 *The OC Domain is rich with managerial and cash related metrics that provide at least as much, if not more information that managers feel they're getting from their cost accounting information*

	Definition	Metrics
Buy	Purchasing capacity or transactions Meeting obligations such as taxes and royalties	Business cash requirements (BCR) Input capacity Accounts payable
Consume	The rate of using capacity to perform work	Effeciency Capacity consumption Capacity utilization Capacity availability
Create	Output created from performing work	Effectivity Productivity Output capacity Units of output
Sell	Output sold to that should lead to recenue and offset	Offset Demand Receivables

Buy

With the buy category, the focus is on cash$_{OUT}$; understanding how much money is being spent, the rate it is being spent, on what, and future cash obligations that are created as a result of the timing of the purchase and the payment terms. The key metrics are business cash requirements or BCR, input capacity, and accounts payable.

BCR was covered in more detail in the last chapter. The value represents the amount of cash that leaves the organization and the cumulative amount of cash that has left the company over any combination of analysis periods. This is a baseline metric that creates clarity regarding the rate of spend and how much revenue is necessary to break even.

Input capacity reflects the amount of capacity you've purchased. This includes labor, space, materials, and equipment that you've paid for and have available for use. Paying for it affects BCR.

Payables focuses on all pending payment expectations. This is important when projecting BCR or understanding the impact of an investment or management decision on BCR. Payables in the OC Domain expands to include all payments including all capacity costs, rather than that for which the company may be billed or invoiced as considered in the Accounting Domain. This makes payables in the OC Domain much larger and impactful than it is in the Accounting Domain.

Consume

Consume focuses on how, and the extent to which capacity is being used. There are four primary metrics available to analyze consumption. These are efficiency, capacity consumption, capacity utilization, and capacity availability.

Efficiency gets an undeserved bum rap by many management gurus. Efficiency is just a value with no judgment involved. It is like the speed reading on a speedometer. The speedometer doesn't tell you whether you should speed up or slow down. It just provides you with a value. Mathematically, efficiency is the ratio of output to input. If you get more output with the same input, or you get the same output with less input, you've become more efficient. Generally speaking, operating efficiently should be a fundamental objective of all managers. The primary way you make more money is by managing and improving efficiency, but only to a point.

The bum rap comes from individuals and companies that have created problems by trying to exploit the efficiency value or number. Forcing people to work unnecessarily hard, working in bad conditions, using cheap materials, over producing, and over buying may all result from a drive to be as efficient as possible. Setting artificially high efficiency targets, which are often arbitrary, may drive this undesirable behavior. These aren't efficiency issues, they're managerial issues. Blaming these decisions on efficiency is like blaming running red lights on trying to improve gas mileage. Running red lights may improve your gas mileage because you aren't sitting there getting zero miles per gallon, but it is still a dumb thing to do.

If you choose to use cheap materials to become more efficient and the result is that your product fails in the market, that's not an efficiency issue, it's a management issue. That is a failure to use the metric in the proper context. Part of the context that helps curb bad decision making as it relates to efficiency is provided with two metrics covered later in this chapter; effectiveness and productivity. Focusing solely on efficiency in the absence of being effective and productive can be highly destructive.

Consumption tells you how much capacity was used by a product, service, activity, or when performing general work. Consumption uses the same units as the capacity you buy. For example, a meeting may consume four of eight hours you bought, or offices consume 3,000 of the 4,000 square feet you leased. Consumption is actually a key input to calculated costs and can, in many cases, serve as a proxy for calculated costs but with greater managerial value because it has not been transformed into a cost.

Capacity utilization tells us two things. First, it helps us understand what percentage of the capacity we've purchased is or has been consumed. If underutilized, you may be paying for more capacity than you need. If it's close to 100 percent utilized, it is likely you will either need more, you need to reduce the demand, or increase your efficiency so that output requires less capacity. This will allow you to minimize the inherent risks of running resources at close to 100 percent for extended periods, which can lead to breakdowns. Second, proper capacity utilization tells us what is consuming the capacity. Ideally, we'd like to know what demands are being placed on the capacity so that we can work to manage capacity levels as necessary. Finally, utilization helps us understand how much capacity is available for use.

Capacity availability helps us understand how much input capacity we may have available for consumption. This is important both when taking on new opportunities and determining whether we can take on an opportunity without making an additional investment in capacity. For instance, hospitals may not want to maintain 100 percent capacity use, because it limits their ability to take in new patients who need their services. Some companies want to make sure capacity is available for their better, higher paying customers. Finally, when taking on new business, if additional investments in capacity are required, this could have a negative effect on the amount of money you'll make even if the opportunity is accounting-wise profitable. For instance, if an order comes in and you have to buy additional material to fill the order because there is none available, this will affect cash but may have no effect on gross margin.

Create

Create looks at the output and output potential you have, and the amount of output you have created. It's important to recognize all types of operation and process output. We tend to gravitate toward more tangible types of output such as widgets. However, personnel hires, reports, and managerial decisions are all forms of output that consume capacity. There are five primary Create metrics: demand, effectivity, productivity, output/output rate, and output capacity.

Demand focuses on how much work or output is required. This term, however, can often be dangerous when left up to interpretation. Demand is your interpretation of what the consumer wants and commits to. There is an artificial demand that is created outside of actual demand. Sometimes this is used in situations such as forecasting sales. However, it can also lead to bad managerial decision making. The key is to focus on what you believe is real and highly likely to occur. When not being diligent about understanding and managing artificial demand, overproduction or finding work for which there is no consumer demand to improve capacity utilization often results. This may cause companies to create and keep higher capacity levels than necessary.

Effectivity, as defined here, considers whether the right output has been created. This is a comparison of output to demand for specific, useable output. For instance, there is a market for black pens and I make black pens. This is being effective. The effective use of capacity involves creating output for which there is demand. Capacity is ineffective if it is used to create the wrong type of output or when it creates defective output. For example, I decide to make orange pens even though the only market is for black pens.

Productivity, in this book and within BDM, represents an alignment of output levels with demand. If you are effective and efficient, but you create more output than there is demand for, you are overproductive. If you produce less than demand, you are underproductive. To clarify, being ineffective means making the wrong things. Being over or underproductive means you are making too much or not enough of the right thing. Producing 25 black pens when there is only demand for 20 may be efficient and effective, but it is overproductive. Making 18 black pens is underproductive. Making 25 orange pens may be efficient, but it is neither effective or productive.

These three metrics in essence, balance each other and help keep companies focused on creating output at levels that are consistent with demand. If there is demand for 20 black pens, we should produce 20. Focusing too much on efficiency will cause you to overproduce or to use capacity ineffectively. Failures in each of the three will cause you to spend more on capacity or to forego revenue opportunities.

I hear people talking about achieving the highest level of efficiency possible. This is a mistake in my mind. The approach that should be taken would be to optimize efficiency. The difference can be subtle to some, so let me explain. The term "optimization" has been highjacked by consultants. I hear consultants regularly talking about optimizing something when they really only seek to improve it, or they talk about optimizing something without considering constraints.

Optimization is a particular approach to problem solving that seeks to find absolute maximum or minimum solutions in the face of constraints; factors that may keep you from to generating the absolute best solution. For instance, one objective might be to minimize drive time to from Atlanta, Georgia to Orlando Florida, subject to the facts that you can't drive over 35 miles per hour, you must take 15 minute breaks every hour, and you must fill up on gas a minimum of three times during the trip. The clearly this isn't the fastest way to get to Orlando driving, as there is a freeway that connects the two cities. However, sometimes there are conditions that must be met, and so optimization seeks the best possible solution given the existence of these conditions.

The anatomy of an optimization problem is that there is an objective for which you'd like to find the absolute maximum or minimum (shortest time), and constraints that limit those values (35 mph, three gasoline stops, 15 minute breaks every hour). When it comes to efficiency, there are two ways to consider the metric. The first is to come up with the maximum efficiency without constraints. This might mean effectivity and productivity be damned; whether we need the output or not, we will keep working to improve efficiency. A better way is to consider effectivity and productivity as constraints; maximize efficiency subject to the following: effectivity must equal 100 percent, meaning all output was the same type as demand, productivity must equal 100 percent suggesting that you not only made the right stuff, but you did so in the right amounts, and employees spend 8 hours per week on improvement activities of their choice.

Like the trip to Orlando, better numbers could be created without the constraints, but the constraints often exist for a reason. Efficiency for efficiency's sake can be detrimental to your firm, so it must be managed in the context of appropriate business practices and objectives.

A sine qua non for calculating efficiency, effectiveness, and productivity is output. Output represents work that has been or is in the process of being created. It might be how many R&D trials are underway or completed. It could be the number of invoices processed. It could also be widgets or treated patients. Output rate adds a time and, therefore, speed element to output. Twenty invoices is output. Twenty invoices per day or week is output rate, suggesting the speed at which output is created.

Output capacity is the final key metric. Output capacity represents how much output potential you have. For instance, someone working for an hour and has the potential to make eight telemarketing calls in that hour has an output capacity of eight calls per hour even though the output rate may be seven. The ratio of the two is capacity utilization.

The temptation is to attempt to achieve 100 percent capacity utilization. The belief is that if you have capacity, it should be used. However, recall, whether we use capacity or not has no impact on what we paid for it. That someone calculates a *cost* of a certain amount per unit time when capacity sits idle, for instance, has no validity from a cash cost perspective. It may become an issue if you have a significant amount of capacity that is grossly underutilized, because this may represent an oversupply of capacity. However, in general, it doesn't matter from a $cash_{OUT}$ perspective whether you're consuming capacity or not. Think of it this way. Does your company's lease payment change with how much warehouse space you're using? No. If it is unused, perhaps it shouldn't have been leased, but that is another issue. If you sit at your desk and accomplish nothing because you don't feel well or are having a bad day, your salary doesn't change.

Hence, a key caution is this. When you don't understand that unused capacity doesn't affect money, you may be tempted to overuse it. A machine is down, for instance, so we must make stuff, even if it causes us to be ineffective and unproductive and possibly spend more cash. People are idle, so we have to make them do something, anything. This approach will not change $cash_{OUT}$, and can lead to capacity over-utilization. When the capacity is people, it can lead to burnout and turnover, all in the name of a cash-wise meaningless metric.

Sell

There are three key metrics when it comes to the sell function in the OC Domain. Those are offset, receivables, and productivity.

Offset is the difference between money that has crossed the CICO Border into the company (cash revenue) and BCR. When offset is positive, the company has made money and when it is negative, the company has lost money. Offset is basically another word for cash profit. Cumulative offset gives you a longitudinal look at cash performance. If, over several periods, cumulative offset is positive, that suggests the company has made money over that period. For instance, if it's November and your fiscal year ends in December, cumulative offset will create a clear and unambiguous picture of how much offset you will need to generate in December to break-even or achieve targets set for the year. Additionally, greater offset in any given period helps offset deficits in past and future periods.

In my work, I use offset instead of accounting profit. My firm has a guarantee: "We will make you more money or we will return your what you paid." With all revenue at risk, understanding where to focus our recommendations and how to create and monitor improvements from a cash perspective becomes imperative. Offset, then, becomes the most effective way I've found to determine and project the cash improvements I, or others, may suggest and implement.

Receivables focuses on the rate and expected timing of revenues expected to be received from all sources by the firm. This helps with projections of cash in both current and future periods.

Productivity creates clarity when considering how much output you have versus how much output was sold. Large differences indicate situations where the firm is potentially losing money. When overproductive, there is a chance more capacity than necessary was bought or consumed to create unnecessary output. When underproductive, the suggestion is that there are sales that are being missed out on because not enough capacity was available to meet the demand for it.

Ultimately, all key operational and financial data reside, natively, in the OC domain. Exhibit 15.1 shows a few examples of the data and information available in the OC Domain without calculating a single cost.

Cost: Spend = BCR

Revenue: cash$_{IN}$

Profit/did we make money: Offest

Production rate: Output

Product, service, customer profitability: Efficiency

Capacity

Capacity consumption

Efficiency

Effectivity

Demand

Overproductive/underproductive

Capacity to meet demand

Excess capacity consumed/Extra capacity required

Excess capacity purchased

Target spend

Potential increase in cash profit by improving effectivity and productivity

Exhibit 15.1 *These are a few examples of the significant amount of cost and managerial data and information that are available from the OC Domain without calculating a single cost*

CHAPTER 16

Conflict Between the OC and Accounting Domains

Back in Chapters 3 and 4, I mentioned BDM is a two-dimensional approach designed to model and manage cash, align operations and accounting, and to manage profitability. Companies typically manage financial information in one-dimension, the Accounting Domain. If the Accounting Domain is one dimension, think of the OC Domain as a separate, yet non-orthogonal dimension.[1] Being another dimension, the OC Domain can highlight, and offer a different perspective of things that you can't see when limited to the Accounting Domain alone. Think about the fact we knew nothing about the 3-D ball when living in the world of the 2-D table in Chapter 4. Concepts and metrics, too, are quite different across the two domains, meaning how they behave and the information they tell us are different in each domain, and in some cases, they are in direct conflict with each other. This means you'll need understanding and clarity, and an approach for prioritization and governance in place to ensure you make the right decision when the concepts do conflict across domains. Here are a few examples of conflicts, some of which we've touched on previously:

- Fixed and Variable Costs
- Contribution Margins
- Profit and Making Money
- Cost Reductions

---

[1] Orthogonal basically means at right angles or independent of one another. For example, front-back is at a right angle to left-right and up-down. The OC Domain and Accounting Domain are not mathematically orthogonal. The idea is to provide a loose metaphor to think about how the domains behave in relation to one another.

- Pricing
- Make versus Buy

Fixed and Variable Costs

I often get into discussions that focus on fixed and variable costs. There is a distinct difference between what is fixed and what varies when comparing the OC Domain costs to Accounting Domain costs. In fact, in some cases, they are the complete opposite.[2] In accounting, variable costs vary with volume. As volume increases, costs increase. The most common types of variable costs are direct materials and direct labor, capacity that is directly involved with creating products or delivering services. As you make more, it follows, your labor and material costs will increase in the Accounting Domain.

Compare this to the OC Domain. In the OC Domain, costs vary with how much you buy, not how you use them. Hence, output and volume don't affect what you pay for the capacity. What you pay for labor and space changes when you buy more, which may be indirectly influenced by volume, but the two are not directly correlated. There are certain thresholds where you may need to increase output capacity such as when demand is greater that your current output capacity. Otherwise, demand is fulfilled with current capacity with no changes to $cash_{OUT}$. In some cases, increasing output capacity means buying more input capacity, but the change in cash is solely based on the decision and subsequent act of buying, not the need to buy. If you need more space and you buy more space, your space costs increase. If you need space, and through the use of lean, for instance, you improve space utilization and you no longer need to buy additional space, cash costs remain unchanged.

When it comes to fixed and variable costs, there are two key factors to consider. The first is, costs that increase directly with volume are $cost_{NC}$. They increase because, since $cost_{NC}$ is an opinion of the value of consumed capacity, when more capacity is consumed, the value of the

---

[2] Lee, R.T. May-June 2016. "Fixed and Variable Costs: When Accounting Is the Opposite of Cash Flow Reality." *Journal of Corporate Accounting & Finance* 27, no. 4, pp. 31–35.

capacity consumed increases. If we calculate a $cost_{NC}$ of $30 for you to perform a task, performing it twice has a $cost_{NC}$ of $60.

The second factor is understanding the dynamics of *why* costs change. With $cost_C$, the only reason it changes is because what you have paid for changes; you bought more or less input or the price of what you've bought has changed.

When in discussions with executives, I find it helps to ask for clarity when talking about costs, because they usually start off in mixed domain mode. When they mention costs, I often ask if we're referring to cash costs, $cost_C$, or accounting/calculated costs, $cost_{NC}$. With accounting costs, the cost itself can increase or decreases with no change in cash costs. For instance, a laborer who goes from making the 6th unit to the 7th unit in the same hour they're getting paid for will increase total costs and reduce unit costs in the Accounting Domain, but nothing happens in the OC Domain. Conversely, cash costs can increase with no increase in $cost_{NC}$. If you place an order for more materials, you will increase your cash costs without changing how the materials are allocated to the product once used.

Contribution Margins

Contribution margin calculations in the Accounting Domain involve attempting to calculate the cash contribution each sale makes. The basic concept is, costs, in the Accounting Domain, are basically either fixed or variable as mentioned in the previous section. Let's say you produce an item with a calculated cost of $3 and you break down the fixed and variable components of the $3; the fixed component is $2, and the variable is $1. A key assumption with contribution margins is, the fixed cost exists anyway, so if you take it out of the equation, you're left with the price and the variable cost of what was sold. When you subtract the variable cost from the price, the difference is believed to represent the cash made on the transaction. A product that has a selling price of $5 with a variable cost of $1, has an assumed $4 in cash as a contribution margin.

Of course, there is "all kinds of wrong" with this. First, the variable cost isn't cash, it's $cost_{NC}$. This means subtracting it from cash makes no sense either mathematically or notionally. Pickup trucks and trees.

Second, the majority of the costs that go into accounting variable costs are capacity costs, so labor and materials don't vary, cash-wise, with volume. Hence, the contribution margin metric doesn't represent the behavior of cash. Third, when creating accounting images, a significant portion of cash costs that need to be offset are left out of the calculus. This is important when trying to figure out how much cash the company needs. For instance, when calculating product costs, HR and executive suite costs are areas not often found in a product's costing algorithm, yet they exist, contribute to BCR, and must be offset with cash. How big are they? How much contribution do we need to create positive offset? Since accounting doesn't use BCR, there is no insight into how much cash is necessary for all sales to offset. Without this information, even if contribution margins did represent cash, without knowing how much is needed to create positive offset, its effectiveness would be limited.

In the OC Domain, contribution margins are a different animal. There, they represent net $cash_{IN}$ (Equation 16.1) Each transaction generates revenue. Sometimes, to get this revenue, you have the capacity to deliver the product or service without incurring any additional cash costs. Hence, $cash_{OUT}$ basically remains the same (consider the MRI example). Someone places the order and you have the wherewithal to fulfill it without buying additional capacity. Other times, you may need to spend money on the outside to achieve the revenue. For instance, you may have bought materials, hired someone, or brought in a service provider with a particular skill or product that can help you deliver to your customers. When you have the capacity, practically all of the revenue goes toward generating offset. If you don't have the ability to deliver, the amount of revenue that goes toward offset is reduced by what you had to spend on materials, additional labor, or other external sources to deliver the work.

$$\text{Net } cash_{IN} = \text{Revenue} - \Delta \, cash_{OUT} \tag{16.1}$$

Consider the following example. Let's say you provide storage as a solution cloud offering. If a company comes to you to buy 50 terabytes of storage, you will have a price, say, $100 per month. Now, how much money will you make off the transaction? In the Accounting Domain, you will have an idea of what the $cost_{NC}$ is to provide this service. Let's say it's $40 and $30 of it is considered variable. The belief is that the company will make $70 in contribution margin.

In the OC Domain, the first question is, do we have the ability to deliver this order with current capacity, or will we need to spend money on any part of the organization to take on this work? For instance, what if there is not enough storage capacity to take on the work? The company will need to spend $3,000 to buy a new server. This increases BCR. The terms will determine when the cash hit happens, but as much as $3,000 may be due immediately. Restating, to get this $100 per month work, an investment of $3,000 is required. If the contract is for 12 months, for the year, revenue is $1,200 and the change in cash$_{OUT}$ was $3,000. Although the opportunity was profitable in the Accounting Domain, it lost money for the year in the OC Domain.

If the objective is to understand how much cash an order creates, where does this show up in the Accounting Domain? The accounting impact of the $3,000 will not hit the income statement directly, so it's impact on accounting profit won't be nearly as drastic as its impact on cash profit. This suggests accounting contributions create an incomplete cash picture.

Profit and Making Money

In the Accounting Domain, profit, specifically gross profit, is really the difference between revenue and the value of capacity consumed. Assume you have two products that both sell for $5. If product A's cost is $2, suggesting it consumed $2 worth of capacity, and product B's cost is $3, Product A is considered more profitable than B. Because the perception of profit is so grand and pervasive, companies put lots of effort into reducing the cost of products such as B, so they can improve profit—the amount of money they believe they're making. In *Profit beyond Measure*, Johnson talks about how much money and effort was expended by the Big Three to reduce unit costs by buying bigger and faster production equipment, all in an effort to reduce costs. In the end, rather than making money through improved gross margins, they ultimately just improved their efficiency on a micro scale (departments and factories) and not on a macro scale (the company).

Another set of decisions that result from profit analyses in the Accounting Domain, is determining profitable customers and profitable products/service lines. The calculus is the same as before. Customer A buys the same product as customer B, but because customer B is "high maintenance," they consume more of your capacity than A. The "cost to serve" B is calculated to be higher suggesting they are less profitable than A. The products A and B buy are basically the same but made for different markets. However, due to the market segment Product B serves, it is perceived to have "higher costs" because of the customer service incidents and capacity consumption that happen with B but not A. Because B consumes more capacity, it has a higher cost and is, therefore, considered less profitable than A.

In the OC Domain, these situations are looked at much differently. Every product is the result of output created by input. The output creates that which was sold, and the inputs are the capacity bought, paid for, and consumed. These are the components that comprise efficiency.

$$\text{efficiency} = \text{output} \div \text{input} \qquad (16.2)$$

Product A $5 output, consumes $2 worth of input capacity (input). For the same $5, Product B consumes $3 worth of input capacity. A is more efficient than B. This approach does not posit whether money is being made or lost; just that one consumes more, or more expensive capacity, than the other. In the same way and using practically the same data, efficiency allows you to look at how much capacity was consumed and compare products and services just like profit analyses without relying on a calculated cost. The benefit is, these two situations may generate the same offset regardless of efficiency, so you are not lulled into thinking you're losing money by keeping a certain product or customer and eliminating the offering leading to no offset being generated at all. If one product consumes more capacity than the other, this becomes an opportunity to improve the capacity utilization of that customer or product as you attempt to bring it in line with others.

Ultimately, efficiency gives you the same information as unit costs. The way this happens mathematically is, cost per unit considers the cost of the input, often capacity, and divides it by units. An example is, when calculating average costs, one takes a cost such as labor and divides it by unit as we do with isocash curves. In this case, we take the $25 for an hour of labor and divide it by output. The resulting ratio is,

$$\text{cost/unit} = \text{input capacity} \div \text{output capacity} \qquad (16.3)$$

In the OC Domain, to calculate efficiency, you take the output capacity and divide it by the input capacity. The $25 and the one hour of work are input capacity and the output is what was created in the hour you bought. Notice, same numbers and same data. Cost per unit is just the reciprocal, or math inverse, of efficiency without the drama. For instance, with efficiency, every improvement leads to an equivalent increase in efficiency. Going from two units to three is the same improvement as going from three to four, or from 1,000 to 1,001. However, when considering the isocost curve, going from two to three yields a greater savings per unit than from three to four or from 1,000 to 1,001. Ask yourself, what is the business implication of this phenomenon?

Reducing accounting cost per unit does not mean you are saving cash. It's just means you're using your capacity more efficiently. This also suggests, although certain customers or products may be more profitable from an accounting perspective, it does not mean you make more money from them. The offset may, in fact, be exactly the same.

Aside from the drama from the isocash curve, there is another key reason why product/service/customer efficiency is a better idea than profitability. When someone equates profit to money, they assume less profit is less money, no profit is no money, and negative profit is losing money. A funny example I once heard was what the controller of a consulting firm said about one of their customers, "When they call, and we pick up the phone, we've already lost money." This is the controller and he actually believed that because a certain customer called and the people they paid to be there answer the phone, money was lost!

This notion that profit is money is not necessarily true when considered from the OC Domain. First, again, there is the bad math issue; money – opinion of values ≠ money. Pickup trucks and trees. Second, the resources are capacity. There is no cost associated with consuming capacity, performing tasks, and creating output. Hence, the customer who demands attention from leaders, sales, and customer service may consume more resources, but that is not money.

I've seen too many examples of this situation going south quickly. Overzealous consultants and analysts perform a customer profitability analysis and then recommend that their customer "rationalize" their unprofitable or low profit customers. What you lose, in this case, is the revenue from these customers that contributes to offset. Unless you eliminate all capacity associated with the account, meaning all people, space, equipment and so on., their cash costs still contribute to BCR while the revenue turned away is not offsetting BCR. Hence, you lose the revenue from having them there while maintaining the capacity cost structure. This is a recipe for losing money.

Another key difference between Accounting Domain profit and OC Domain profit is, Accounting Domain profit doesn't follow rules that cash should follow. Recall, matching and accruals allows for the consideration of past and future cash transactions that fall outside the analysis period. This, of course, is not allowed from a cash perspective.

The most effective way to determine if you are making money is to calculate offset in the OC Domain. It is unperturbed by transformations and you have full integrity with capacity, the primary source of OC Domain cash expenditures. You will also understand how the data are transformed into accounting information, which creates context for the reports that are created in the Accounting Domain.

Cost Reductions

When you think about cost reductions, you typically think about increasing profit; making more money. However, this isn't always the case. If we think about ways we typically reduce costs, it usually involves getting more output from resources or reducing the amount of effort involved in an action, activity, or task. For instance, if a $25 per hour employee increases their output from 20 in an hour to 25, they average cost per unit of output goes from $1.25 down to $1 (Exhibit 16.1) We also see this if we say the average task takes three minutes. At $25 per hour, an assumption is that each minute is worth 41.67¢. A task that uses three minutes of capacity would cost $1.25. Now, let's assume we can take this task time

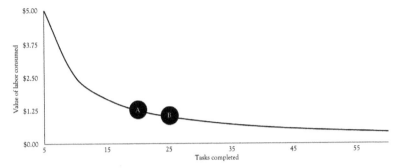

Exhibit 16.1 *Moving from A to B by increasing output gives the impression costs have gone down. While cost$_{NC}$ goes down, cost$_C$ functions increase monotonically, suggesting cash costs never go down with increased output*

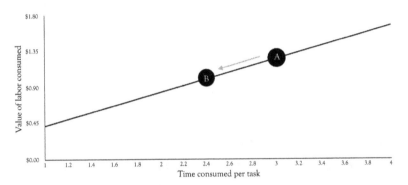

Exhibit 16.2 *Going from A to B will give the perception that unit costs have gone down. Most improvements that focuses on reducing process/operation time will look like this. Although the improvement consumes less capacity, cash has not changed*

down from three minutes to 2.4 minutes. This translates to a cost of $1 for the task. We can see, in both cases, cost reduction associated with the improvement (Exhibit 16.2).

In both situations, costs have gone down in the Accounting Domain suggesting improved profit and more money. However, the changes are to cost$_{NC}$ and they have no direct effect on cash at all. The amount of input capacity purchased remains the same, so the cash$_{OUT}$ remains the same. In the first example, the improvement in efficiency, output ÷ input, moves you down the same isocash curve. Additionally, when reducing the amount of time consumed for work, you are still on the same isocash curve.

This is more proof you can reduce costs without affecting cash flow. In the OC Domain, cost reductions only happen by affecting $cash_{OUT}$. From a capacity perspective, this means buying less input capacity, buying cheaper input capacity, or some combination of both. By doing so, you are moving to a lower isocash curve, suggesting less money is leaving the company.

Pricing

In the Accounting Domain, the focus of pricing is to ensure the company meets desired margins. One very common way companies attempt to do this is to calculate a cost, add a margin to it, and that becomes the selling price. For instance, it you want to make $1.50 on an item you've calculated to cost $3, the price would be $4.50. This technique is called cost plus pricing, and much to the chagrin of many pricing professionals, it's practically a standard approach for many companies.

Cost plus pricing fails in many ways. First, as has been stated a number of times before, the $3 calculated cost isn't unique. It can be anything. Using a different scope for the analysis or a different transformation algorithm, that number could have been $2.17, $1.25, or $6.22 just as easily as it could be $3, so how do you know you're "making" $1.50? Second, the $3 is not cash. Third, the approach does not consider the value of the product or service to the customer. For example, what if the value of the aforementioned product to the customer is $7 rather than the $4.50? The company is leaving an additional $2.50 on the table every time one is sold. What may be worse is, because of the perceived discounted price, the demand may increase because the price seems like such a bargain. Consumers buy more, and you're happy you're getting your margins. All the while, you may be compromising your cash because you may be bringing in less overall revenue. Additionally, if your calculated cost is affected by volume, increases in volume may call for lower prices since you're farther out on the isocash curve and your cost per unit may be lower. You may now think you can still make $1.50 with a $4 versus $4.50 selling price.

This may lead to even smaller revenue generating opportunities which, of course, compromises offset.

The flip side to this is when your price is too high for the market. If the market is only willing to pay $4 for the product and you turn down the business, you may be turning away an opportunity to generate offset as in the MRI example. If you are at or near full capacity and there are people who are waiting and willing to pay $4.50 or more, it makes sense to turn away the business at $4. However, if you have idle capacity, selling the item generates revenue which improves offset.

Another approach related to pricing that is an Accounting Domain issue is target costing. The idea is, the market will ultimately determine your price. Understanding the market will only pay $4.50 for your product, you decide each manufactured product can't cost more than $3.00. Engineers will then look for ways to improve the design and manufacture of the product, so it comes in at, or below, the $3.00 target.

Target costing is an interesting notion, but it's really no different from any other cost-plus approach except it forces discipline with respect to the factors that affect cost. Setting a $3.00 target is just an idea that helps designers, engineers and manufacturing personnel focus and improve input capacity utilization and output capacity. The numbers they focus on to reduce costs are really just improving efficiency. This exercise won't necessarily save money in and of itself, and in some cases, it may hurt. By reducing product costs, you report a higher unit income. The higher income may cause you to have to pay higher taxes.

In the OC Domain, the objective is to maximize net revenue (net cash$_{IN}$). The maximum revenue comes from value pricing, where the price is aligned with what the customer is willing to pay. Subtracted from this are any expenditures, not accounting variable costs, involved in providing the particular service; the cash contribution versus the accounting contribution discussed earlier in the chapter. This difference will be the amount of net revenue you have to pay off BCR and generate offset. One customer called it giving back to the kitty. The net revenue is a key value and suggests contribution is not a fixed amount. There may be times getting business may require investments in capacity that affect net revenue and other times, it will not. The revenue will be the same, but the net revenue may change. This suggests you should consider all changes in cash$_{OUT}$ that increase BCR and their long term implications when taking on new business. This should happen in lieu of accounting margins if the focus is on money.

Make Versus Buy

Make versus buy analyses can be highly misleading. As mentioned in Chapter 1, the idea is to determine whether it is cheaper to make or perform a service or buy it from the outside. The first challenge to this approach is, the analysis compares apples and oranges. Your calculated cost (apples) is not cash. Buying from the outside (oranges) is cash, so you are trying to compare two dissimilar things as if they were the same. Second, unless you eliminate all capacity related to what you outsource, residual capacity will remain leading to the possibility of actually increasing BCR rather than decreasing it. This might happen because you are still paying for the initial capacity, and now you're spending more to buy from the outside, as we saw with the university copy example in Chapter 14.

This chapter has focused on managerial and financial differences between the two domains. They sometimes conflict. This is why it's important to understand how both domains interpret common situations, so you don't, unknowingly, sub optimize your organization.

Now, let's discuss improvement projects such as lean and IT, and how to ensure you realize cash-based benefits from implementing them.

CHAPTER 17

Improvement Projects

An area in management where using BDM concepts should be front and center is with improvement activities. Whether reducing product, service, or activity costs, or going through a significant improvements or transformations enabled by lean, Six Sigma, or IT, the objective is to improve how much money we make. In fact, Taiichi Ohno, the architect of the Toyota Production System (TPS), the precursor to lean, argued the primary role of TPS was cost reduction with the hope of improving how much money Toyota made.[1]

Each year, executives around the world spend billions on improvements they feel will make their departments, divisions, or companies more money, and they walk away disappointed. I believe there are three key reasons this happens.

1. Cash is tied to input capacity
2. Improvements are tied to output capacity
3. Companies fail to convert the improvements in output capacity to reductions in input capacity

Let's look at each.

Input and Cash

As mentioned throughout the book, we spend money to buy input capacity. The rate of spend affects $cash_{OUT}$ which, in turn, influences BCR. With the input capacity we buy, we establish the basis for being able to create output capacity. Buying office space enables us to establish offices where people can do their work.

---

[1] Ohno, T. 1988. *Toyota Production System: Beyond Large Scale Production*, 8. Cambridge, MA: Productivity Press.

Improvements

Most improvements affect efficiency. For instance, simplifying or automating operations may allow for less capacity to be consumed when creating output. They may also help the same capacity create more output. Either way, the result is either more output with the same input or same output while consuming less input. However, if the input is a person whose time is being bought and where money is spent, the overall input is not affected. If someone reduces the time it takes you to do something, your salary isn't adjusted.

Those designing these improvements often capture cost savings here. For instance, consuming one fewer hour of a $30 per hour resource will "save" $30. As we've seen, this value is $cost_{NC}$, so it is not cash. An extreme case involved a healthcare executive who, in a discussion, quoted a $7,000 cost for each day a patient stayed in their hospital. His thought was, by reducing the number of patient-days by 1,000, the hospital could save seven million dollars.

This is a major flaw with business cases and cash-benefit analyses developedthis way. The cost savings, in many cases, are $cost_{NC}$ and not $cost_C$ savings. Hence, the comparison and subsequent return on investment (ROI) is not valid from a cash perspective. The $5M promised by an IT consultant resulting from a software implementation may be a $5M reduction in capacity consumption value, but it quite frequently is not $5M in cash. The ROI analyses of company savings and spend in cases like these are no longer valid. You cannot calculate an ROI, for instance, by comparing $5M in non-cash dollars to $1M in cash dollars and believe you have a 4:1 ROI. The numerator, savings – investment, is mathematically invalid because they're different values; pickups and trees.

The danger is, most do not realize this. They identify false cash savings and claim victory. These saving will not be realized in cash because they are not cash. Time and time again, I've been asked to review value propositions software companies and consultants promise only to find that the savings promised were oftentimes off by an order of magnitude or more from a cash savings perspective. In other words, the $10M in savings promised by the consultants *may* yield $1M in cash.

Realizing the Savings

The objective should be to reduce $cost_C$ not $cost_{NC}$ when looking to improve your cash position. This means converting the efficiency improvement into cash savings by shifting to a different isocash curve. The way this happens is, the efficiency improvement will free input capacity. For instance, if, in eight hours, a worker can process or produce 56 widgets and a productivity improvement allows her to now do it in seven hours, she has one extra hour that is available. Leaving this situation alone means $cost_C$ is still the same if she is paid for eight hours, and no money was saved. Only when you buy one less hour of her time has $cost_C$ changed.

I'm not advocating for companies to start cutting staff, however. I am very much pro employment and look for ways to keep and hire people rather than cut them. In this case, I'm only the messenger. If you want to make money by reducing costs, you do so by buying less. Spending the same whether she takes seven or eight hours to make the widgets leads to no money savings. This is what many companies leave out of their analyses and implementation plans; converting efficiency savings into cash savings. Four steps will help make this happen:

1. Determine impact of improvement on output capacity
2. Identify steps necessary to achieve these savings
3. Determine how $cash_{OUT}$ will change as a result of the capacity savings
4. Create and execute an implementation plan

Impact on Capacity Levels

The first step in calculating the impact is documenting the improvement on output capacity consumption. Recall from Chapter 15, capacity consumption is the amount of capacity units output consumes. Any improvement should have projections of how operations and processes will be better, whether point projections or a range, that should be achieved from implementing the solution. For instance, with our worker, the improvement allowed her to create the same output, 56 widgets, in one less hour. If we do not know the improvement with that level of precision, we may project that she should be able to product somewhere between 54 and 58 widgets in seven hours, or to make 56 widgets somewhere between 6:45 and 7:15 hours. Ranges help immensely in the face of uncertainty.

Document the Steps Necessary

One of the most painful things I experience when helping companies is what I call *if-then* statements; *if* we have better data *then* costs go down or, *if* we implement this software, *then* inventory will be optimized. There is a presumption that improvements just happen. The question is, "*How* will they happen?" What actions, specifically, need to occur? In the case of our worker, what needs to happen before she can create 56 widgets in seven versus eight hours? Implement software alone? Training? Provide her with input faster? Eliminate nonvalue added steps? Eliminate mistakes? In many cases, improvements don't just happen. They must be enabled.

Documenting what is required forces you to think about what you have to do to realize improvements and whether they are actually realizable. As you review these steps, you can do a validation check; if we do these things, will we get her to 56 widgets in seven hours? If not, refine the improvement or the steps necessary to achieve the target and then reassess. Once you agree the steps will achieve the benefit, you now have a checklist to work against.

Document Plan to Save Money

The way to reduce $cost_C$ is to reduce $cash_{OUT}$. The way to do this is to spend less on capacity, transactions, and or TF&R. Here, we'll focus specifically on capacity.

As mentioned in the previous step, improvements should affect output capacity and consumption. If successfully completed, we should have an idea how much of a change to output capacity will occur and what is required to achieve it. The next is to convert that into $cost_C$ savings by reducing $cash_{OUT}$.

The idea with this step is to consider the nature of the improvements to see if you can position yourself to buy less capacity (Exhibit 17.1). For instance, if our worker can make 56 widgets and we are going to pay her

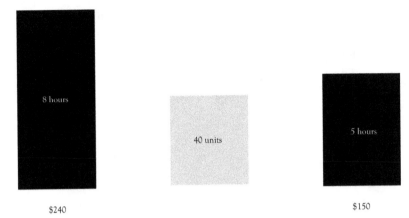

8 hours

40 units

5 hours

$240

$150

Exhibit 17.1 Ultimately, you'd like to pay the lowest level of cash to meet demand, regardless of the source of demand. Paying $150 to sell $2000 worth of services is generally better than paying $240. The key is to ensure you are not overtaxing your company and its capacity to do so. That environment is not sustainable

for eight hours anyway, there won't be any cash savings. However, if there are opportunities to buy less capacity, that is what should be documented as a part of your implementation plan. Consider space reduction. If you can consolidate space, you'll need to figure out which offices or warehouses you will consolidated, when, who has to make the decisions, are they on board, will there be broken leases, if so, are there penalties, how much, and who makes the call? A detailed plan of how the savings in output can be converted into input capacity reduction opportunities which, in turn, need to be turned into a plan of action with steps, names, timing, and approvals identified.

Implementation Plan

These steps create your implementation plan. Once you execute your project, you check off the assumptions as you progress toward achieving the cash$_{OUT}$ improvements. Since you have a detailed description with steps, accountabilities, and anticipated improvements, you can compare reality with what you projected. Variances will inevitably occur. "We were off with our savings projections because we could not convince the leasing company to end the lease early, so we paid for two leases in one month" or "There were resource availability constraints, so we had to delay the start of the improvement." However, instead of this being a negative situation, care should be taken to understand the source of the variance so that lessons learned can be considered to improve future performance.

CHAPTER 18

Capacity Planning and Budgeting

As suggested multiple times previously, demand is one of the most important concepts in BDM. This is because optimal financial performance is achieved at the lowest cost (cost$_C$) to meet demand. If the organization carries too much capacity, its cash$_{OUT}$ will be higher than necessary leading to less cash profit (offset). On the other hand, having too little capacity may create lost opportunities (such as lost sales), may increase risk (work not being completed on time or properly), and in the case of labor and equipment capacity, may create stress on them leading to potential breakdowns or the need to spend in inefficient ways to make up the deficit.

Demand creates context for how efficient, effective, and productive operations are. This is an important element that is critically missing in the Accounting Domain. When you look at the income statement, balance sheet, and cash flow statements, there is no insight into whether you created too much, too little, or just the right amount of output. You may see a gross margin of, say, 40 percent, but that does not reflect the notion that to get that cost, you had to overproduce by 20 percent to achieve it (Exhibit 18.1).

Now, assume there are items in inventory resulting from the overproduction. If you see an increase in asset value on the balance sheet, will you know its source? The answer is, "no." The balance sheet usually doesn't break down inventory by type—raw, work in process, or finished goods—so it, alone, would provide no clues regarding whether the profile of the inventory changed, let alone why it changed.

Finally, consider the cash flow statement. The statement shows *that* you spent money, but not *why* you spent it. It may be broken down into categories such as investing, operating, and financial cash flow, but the specific reason why the money was spent (e.g., ran overtime in the

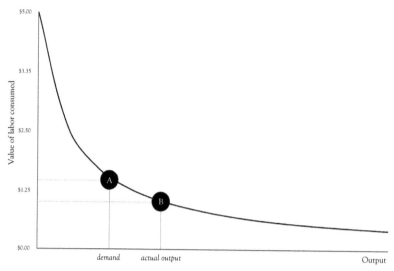

Exhibit 18.1 *This scenario creates the perspective that the company is better off from a margin perspective with increased output, although cash-wise, nothing has changed. These scenarios are dangerous because they lead to overproduction and overbuying in the names of efficiency and reducing costs*

finishing department), and on what is lost. Hence, the three statements will not really help you understand *that* or *why* you're spending too much money and the impact it has on your ability to generate cash profit.

Consider budgeting. Capacity, as noted many times previously, is one of the largest expenditures for most companies. Hence, when budgeting, the key area you should focus on is capacity; how much capacity will you need to buy and pay for? Capacity levels should be dictated by the output required; by demand. However, without projecting the demand for work, how will you know how much capacity you will need? Thus, capacity planning and management is a critical element when looking to plan both current and future activities for budgeting purposes.

The capacity planning process involves five key steps:

1. Determine essential demand;
2. Establish the output levels necessary to meet the essential demand;
3. Determine consumption rates necessary to create the demand levels;

4. Decide how much input you will need to buy to meet the output levels and when;

5. How will the timing of the payments occur for BCR purposes?

Essential Demand

The first step of capacity planning and management begins with essential demand. Essential demand is what we believe to be the truest level of demand for products or services we can quantify. In some industries, it may be orders, which is actual demand. Other industries use forecasts to create a projected demand to address uncertainty. Projected demand should have some rigor involved in determining the value. For instance, if you're an office supply company and you forecast 1000 pencils because it's a nice round number or because sales pulled the number out of a dark place, this is not a true level of demand. You may have never sold more than 900, there is no upward sales trend, and your statistical analyses say the likelihood of exceeding 920 pencils is 0.001 percent. Rigor focuses on trying to determine the minimum demand we can forecast that balances investment in inventory, service levels, and loss of sales in case inventory is not available. This would be your essential projected demand. Sometimes, essential demand will be a combination of both actual and projected demand.

Essential demand isn't limited to external customer demand. Instead, essential demand is the need that output should address regardless of whether the demand is internal or external. For instance, the need to hire employees creates a demand for interviewing capacity. The number of sales orders that have to be input creates demand for sales order entry capacity. In both cases, there may be a real component (five interviews scheduled, or sales orders received), and an artificial component (five scheduled interviews, some may drop out, three more are considering or other rush orders may arrive) to allow for effective capacity planning.

It is important to distinguish essential demand from total demand. Consider the following. Assume there is demand for 10 widgets for today's work based on existing customer orders (actual). You know, from history, other orders come in throughout the day, so you'll need to forecast what this number may be. Although actual demand for your widgets may be 10, you may establish a total demand for 15, forecasting a maximum of five additional orders will come throughout the day. This will help insure against lost revenue or to plan capacity. You may also do this because producing 15 versus 10 with the same inputs increases efficiency. Why you chose 15 should not be ignored. In one case, rigor is involved, and the interest is in finding the right level of demand projecting future demand. The other is an exploitation of metrics, such as emphasizing efficiency or maximizing economies of scale independently of true demand, which should be avoided.

Total demand is the sum of actual and projected demand. The projected demand may or may not have passed the rigor test suggested previously in the pencil example. When it has passed the rigor test, it is essential demand (Exhibit 18.2). It is essential demand that should be the basis for capacity planning.

It's key, therefore, to separate real versus artificial demand so you can calculate essential demand more effectively. Without separating the two types of demand, the perceived total demand, the aggregate of the two may be inflated because artificial demand may have been forecasted or chosen to be higher than necessary or reasonable. This may lead to greater capacity consumption and possibly higher BCR.

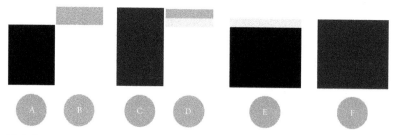

Exhibit 18.2 Point A represents the actual demand—what we have orders for. B is the projected demand, a forecast of what we think we may need above actual demand in this case. C becomes the total demand. Point D represents the rigor test. Not all of the projected demand is likely to occur, so the total is reduced to what is believed to be more likely. Point E shows the sum of the actual and the tested projected demand, leading to an F being the essential demand

Breaking down the demand will allow you to consider how much, if any, of the artificial demand you want to consider as essential demand. For instance, a statistical analysis may suggest although you have actual demand for 10, 99 percent of the time, you can expect no more than two more orders to come in during the period. In that case, you may choose to create 12, instead of 15, so that you can fulfill the total demand for 12. Creating 15, although more efficient would involve being overproductive.

The sum of the real demand and the amount of artificial demand you accept becomes your essential demand. This is what should be used for budgeting and planning purposes. Over time, it'll be important to improve the ability to determine artificial demand with the long term objective being to respond to changes in real demand in industries where this is possible. In some industries, it's impossible. Burger King can't go buy burgers when each customer walks through its doors!

Projecting Demand

Ideally, the demand you will project is essential demand. As with any other projection, there is a loss of precision as time, and the number of unknowns, increase. For instance, you are more likely to know essential demand with a higher degree of precision tomorrow than you will one year from tomorrow.

One tool to use when there is uncertainty is to project a range rather than an actual single value as discussed last chapter. For instance, projecting you will have to process eight customer service calls per day one year from now is more than likely wrong. However, you may be able to project, based on reasonable assumptions, that the demand for calls will fall somewhere between six and 14. When creating your upper and lower bounds, you state the assumptions that would create each boundary to occur. This, then, can be used as a foundation for projecting demand. Might fourteen be more likely than six given the stated assumptions? More likely than eight? If so, you can begin adjusting the demand range based on the likelihood the assumptions come true.

Demand is a critical component when budgeting in a BDM environment. This process helps to determine the likely demand levels so that capacity can be aligned more effectively, which is the next step.

Output

We've spent a significant amount of time on output, so I won't rehash here. The objective with output in the context of planning and budgeting is to align it with demand. This alignment will help set expectations regarding how much output capacity you will have to plan and budget for.

Consumption

Working backwards, the output levels, along with key metrics such as efficiency, effectivity, and productivity will help you determine how much capacity will be needed to create the output to meet demand. For instance, if you need to create 12 widgets per hour to meet essential demand and each person can produce three per hour, you will need to consume the equivalent of four people per hour to create the output. If you need 12 per day at the same rate, you will only need to buy four hours of labor per day. This info will allow for planning capacity levels in the future.

When budgeting, this step helps you identify improvement opportunities. If you are looking to reduce labor, for instance, it will help you understand where and how to focus your efficiency improvement efforts. By increasing the output in the previous example by one unit per hour, you can now meet demand with three people versus four.

Buy

Once you understand the amount of capacity you project you will need, you can back into an amount you should buy by considering your capacity utilization rate. For instance, if you need 1,000 lbs. of useable steel to create salable output and you use 98 percent of what you buy on average, you will need to budget to buy 1,021 lbs. to get 1,000 lbs. of useable output. The same applies to labor, although you'll have to consider this one carefully. Depending on the essential and nonessential demand placed on them, you will have to consider an ideal level of utilization. For instance, if you expect 100 percent of their time during an eight-hour work day be assigned to essential demand, yet nonessential demand (think nonvalue added work) is still expected, you can quickly burn out your staff. However, if you expect your people to be 80 percent utilized and to get their job done requires 6.5 hours of consumption, you'll need just over eight hours to meet the consumption rate. If you strictly work eight hour days, you will either have to improve efficiency, so the 6.5 hour requirement goes down, or adjust the utilization rate.

Timing of Cash

The final step is to set expectations for the timing of cash. This is important when considering BCR projections. For most capacity, the amount and timing are known. For instance, salaries are paid on a regular basis as are rent and equipment payments. You will typically know how much these are and when they will be paid. Others, such as materials, will vary based on the combination of demand rate and the amount of material capacity you have. This creates much of the basis for BCR.

What is important, here, is understanding how and when the amount of capacity will change. When choosing to work overtime, for instance, you'd like to know the additional labor cash costs hit. If you have to pay expedited fees for an order, when might that happen? Sometimes, the impact of these actions in the Accounting Domain aren't readily known. You may, for example, incur $30k in direct labor overtime fees that must be paid in the next pay period. From an Accounting Domain perspective, although you might be able to see this if you look in the right place, most won't see it until it shows up as a variance. Even when it does, the cash impact is lost, and for small businesses, $30K combined with sales that aren't sought to offset the additional $30K, may create a cash hardship for the firm.

Ultimately, budgeting comes down to projecting cash needs. This, of course, means projecting future BCR. BCR starts with forecasting capacity and proper capacity levels are a function of demand, productivity, effectivity, and efficiency. This will, within a reasonable degree of accuracy and precision, help you understand output capacity levels, input capacity levels, and, ultimately, the cash required to buy them.

I wanted to take this opportunity to go back to Dr. Johnson's comments about the managing the means versus results. Recall the optimization conversation from Chapter 15. In that discussion, I mentioned that optimization problems seek a best solution in the face of constraints.

There are two types of optima. The first seeks the best solution to an existing problem. The example might be the Big Three response to offering multiple products. A constraint was machine changeover, so an optimization problem might read, "maximize throughput subject to a 4 hour changeover on the stamping machine in Department 235." That will create what is known as a local maximum; the best solution given that setup. However, what if that setup isn't a given? What if we can change the setup so that we can achieve even greater performance that we can by optimizing our current setup?

This is what Toyota did. Instead of optimizing based on the current situation with long set-ups, they asked other questions. Setups are waste. What if we eliminate setups? Doing this shifted the constraints in the Toyota optimization model, so that their optima exceeded what they would have been had they assumed the constraints were fixed. In other words, they created global vs local optima.

As you budget, you can come up with an optimum based on what you have. However, there may be other, greater optima, available by being willing to take on the constraints from an improvement perspective and reducing or eliminating them. That's often how breakthrough performance happens.

CHAPTER 19

Closing

As I close this book, I'd like to leave you with two points. First, if you want to help your firm make money, focus on money. The Accounting Domain cannot do this because it was not designed to model money. As a result, it is not the tool you should look to for answers and guidance. That is the role of the Operations and Cash Domain. However, the Accounting Domain does play another, very important role. We have to report our results, and in that context, the Accounting Domain should be front and center. Ultimately, to have a comprehensive picture of your organization and the data and information to manage it, you'll need both, and that's the role of Business Domain Management; bringing the two together and maintaining business, managerial, and math integrity between them. The OC Domain is about decisions, judgments, and action. The Accounting Domain is about reporting.

Second, the transformation from accounting-focused analyses to BDM should not be a significant undertaking in and of itself. The objective is to add relatively straightforward concepts, tools, measures, and metrics to help you see your organization much more comprehensively. We shouldn't be looking at brand new software systems, but some of the data in your current ERP system should be looked at as suspect. One CEO asked me to work with their firm as they implemented their ERP system to help them improve their decision making. The one thing I pointed out was, we'll need some of the data before it is transformed. Once it has been transformed, it's too late. We've lost the value.

Thank you for your time and attention.

—Reginald Tomas Lee, 2018

About the Author

Reginald Tomas Lee, PhD, is a professor, author, and corporate advisor in the areas of business domain management, cash profit/ROI, capacity management and supply chain. Reginald is a management professor at Xavier University—Williams College of Business, the president of Business Dynamics & Research, and a senior fellow at VeraSage Institute. Previously, he worked for GM, IBM, and Oracle, and held senior supply chain leadership positions at Sapient and EY. He is the author of four books, including *Lies, Damned Lies, and Cost Accounting* for Business Expert Press. His fifth book, *Project Profitability: How to Select, Justify, and Implement Projects to Achieve Maximum Cash ROI*, scheduled for release in 2019. Reginald has written several dozen articles and white papers and was a featured writer for the *Journal of Corporate Accounting & Finance*. Reginald has advised several leading companies including Bristol Myers Squibb, Burger King, Dell, Disney, DuPont, the Home Depot, Lockheed-Martin, Motorola, Toyota, and UnitedHealth Group.

Reginald has a PhD in mechanical engineering from the University of Dayton.

Index

OTHER TITLES IN THE MANAGERIAL ACCOUNTING COLLECTION

Kenneth A. Merchant, University of Southern California, Editor

- *Revenue Management: A Path to Increased Profits, Second Edition* by Ronald J. Huefner
- *Cents of Mission: Using Cost Management and Control to Accomplish Your Goal* by Dale R. Geiger
- *Sustainability Reporting: Getting Started, Second Edition* by Gwendolen B. White
- *Lies, Damned Lies, and Cost Accounting: How Capacity Management Enables Improved Cost and Cash Flow Management* by Reginald Tomas Lee, Sr.
- *Strategic Management Accounting: Delivering Value in a Changing Business Environment Through Integrated Reporting* by Sean Stein Smith
- *Management Accounting in Support of Strategy: How Management Accounting Can Aid the Strategic Management Process* by Graham S. Pitcher

Announcing the Business Expert Press Digital Library

Concise e-books business students need for classroom and research

This book can also be purchased in an e-book collection by your library as

- a one-time purchase,
- that is owned forever,
- allows for simultaneous readers,
- has no restrictions on printing, and
- can be downloaded as PDFs from within the library community.

Our digital library collections are a great solution to beat the rising cost of textbooks. E-books can be loaded into their course management systems or onto students' e-book readers.
The **Business Expert Press** digital libraries are very affordable, with no obligation to buy in future years. For more information, please visit **www.businessexpertpress.com/librarians**. To set up a trial in the United States, please email **sales@businessexpertpress.com**.

CPSIA information can be obtained
at www.ICGtesting.com
Printed in the USA
FSHW021621301220
77110FS

9 781631 578793